THIS
GREEN

&

PLEASANT
LAND

THIS
GREEN
&
PLEASANT
LAND

PHOTOGRAPHY BY BOB GIBBONS

INTRODUCTION BY JULIAN PETTIFER

SECTION INTRODUCTION BY DICK HORNBY

HAMLYN

THIS GREEN AND PLEASANT LAND

A note on the photography

All the photographs for this book, with a few minor exceptions, were taken during a six-month period between April and September 1989. The aim throughout was to try to show how plants and animals work together or fit into a habitat, rather than simply showing them in isolation as pure portraits. Wildlife, in the widest sense, is so often portrayed as a series of independent colourful species, whereas in reality it is made up of vast numbers of interconnecting species, many of them drab and difficult to identify. Together they form communities, ecosystems and habitats, and it is only by understanding wildlife at this level that we can hope to protect it. Natural habitats, in good condition, are the key to virtually all wildlife conservation and the intention throughout this book has been to portray some of the marvellous variety of habitats that Britain still holds.

For the photography, two camera systems were used. A medium format Fuji GX 680, giving 6 × 8 cm pictures on 120 film, was used for many static pictures; this camera was selected because it offers a range of lens movements that help to maximize the depth of field and many of the habitat pictures were produced using this. For the remainder, Nikon 35 mm equipment was used, allowing more flexibility of lens choice and mobility for active shots like that of the otter. All short focal-length lenses were Nikkors, all longer focal-lengths were Sigma apochromatic telephotos and zooms.

The film used throughout was Kodachrome, for its sharpness and accuracy of colour. Kodachrome 25 was used in the 35 mm equipment (it is not available in 120 size) for most pictures; Kodachrome 64 was used in 120, and in 35 mm for more active pictures; Kodachrome 200 was used very occasionally for birds or mammals in difficult conditions. In my experience, Kodachrome 25 gives a much more accurate rendering of flower and leaf colour than any other film.

1989 was an exceptionally odd year. It was warmer and sunnier than almost any previous year this century. This sounds ideal for photography, though in practice it produced a lot of difficulties. Bright sunny days with clear blue skies do not make for either interesting or detailed habitat pictures and throughout May to July I regularly had to get up before 5 a.m. to obtain interesting light, though even at that time of the morning there was rarely any mist or dew because it was so warm. Nevertheless, there were times when the settled weather helped greatly, and I certainly had not expected so many easy island visits or so many clear views in Scotland!

Many people helped me in the quest for sites and species, and in providing helpful information on when to go. The conservation officers, or equivalents, of virtually all county conservation trusts helped with reserve guides and recommendations, and in addition I am especially grateful to Griff Caldwell, Martin Noble, Paul Toynton, John Watt, Billie Murray, Chris Underwood, Peter Wilson, Colin Pope and others too numerous to mention, and especially to Liz and the boys for putting up with me being away so much.

Dr Bob Gibbons

Title page photograph: an autumn hedgerow in Hampshire, showing mainly ivy, bramble and wild rose hips.

Published by The Hamlyn Publishing Group Limited, a division of the Octopus Publishing Group, Michelin House, 81 Fulham Road, London SW3 6RB

ISBN: 0 600 56773 7

Typeset by Servis Filmsetting Limited, Manchester
Typeface: Century Old Style
Produced by Mandarin Offset
Printed and bound in Hong Kong

CONTENTS

INTRODUCTION

Most people in Britain today acknowledge the conservation ethic and see the growing concern for 'green' issues as a healthy trend in society. Many are interested enough to want to take an active role in conservation but, after recycling their waste and avoiding ozone-damaging aerosols, they are unsure which way to turn. They perceive natural history to be too daunting, requiring a higher degree of application than they are able to invest. This book should convince anyone that our wildlife heritage is worthy of contemplation and enjoyment at any level. One does not need to be able to name every blade of grass to understand the main events which have shaped our wildlife and to see what has to be done to prevent further losses. The following pages provide ample evidence of the beauty of wildlife, the fascination of intricate plant and animal relationships, and the splendour of the British landscape. It should become self-evident that wildlife can play a key role in enhancing the quality of life. Nature conservation should be of concern to everyone. We must ensure not only that the most special features are maintained for posterity but that an adequate spread of everyday plants and animals is maintained throughout the country. Nature reserves have a vital part to play in this but wildlife should also be seen as an incidental and welcome benefit of other land use forms.

The photographs in this book show plants and animals not as a series of portraits but in their natural habitats, in the places that they depend upon for their survival. They demonstrate the great variety in the British landscape, the enormous impact of centuries of land management and how wildlife has adapted and flourished whenever a consistent form of land use has become firmly established in a local area. The pictures reveal much of Britain's attractive wildlife, many providing impressive detail while still conveying the essence of the wonderful places in which they are found.

The text explores the relationship between land use and the natural forces of climate, geology and soils, and explains how wildlife has coped with centuries of change and exploitation. The losses of wildlife have been formidable but many places across the country provide fascinating insights into the riches of times when man was less demanding. *This Green and Pleasant Land* reveals the adaptability and vulnerability of nature. We need to understand how plants and animals react to each other and to man's intervention before we can devise effective conservation programmes. The book draws attention to the habitats which are really special, those which could never be recreated and those which are simply typical of forms of land use that are no longer economic.

Nature never likes to be pigeon-holed or classified. Wildlife communities occur as a continuum, with so many anomalies, intermediates and exceptions that it is often difficult to present a logical account of the variation. Plant communities merge into one another and a great many species happily cross major habitat boundaries. Some plants and animals are associated with communities intermediate between two of the major habitats. Others, such as the house sparrow and the black redstart, are strongly associated with the built-up environment and many more, such as the blackbird, hedgehog and small tortoiseshell butterfly, are commonly found in both man-made and semi-natural habitats. The latter species may be attractive or entertaining but they seldom present major conservation problems and they are incidental to the main theme of this book.

The approach used here of dealing with wildlife in six broad categories of habitat is an artificial yet convenient division. For example, wetlands and uplands are intimately related, and it is impossible to avoid discussing bogs in both chapters; grasslands merge into heathlands, uplands and coastal habitats; and scrub is an important intermediate between grassland and woodland. The six sections provide an acceptable vehicle for conveying the essence of Britain's natural heritage but it should not be forgotten that the most valuable wildlife sites are generally those with a mixture of several habitats, merging and varying in response to natural and man-made forces. The whole is invariably greater than the sum of the parts.

The book is essentially about nature but the word 'natural' suggests a degree of freedom from the hand of man which in truth is very difficult to find anywhere in Britain today. The most natural sites, such as high mountains, wooded gorges and sea cliffs, are highly valued in wildlife conservation but even these have generally been altered in some way by man's actions. The most diverse sites are often those where man has consistently made use of nature's resources. The coppiced woodlands of East Anglia, the chalk downland of Wiltshire and the Thames hay meadows all support a host of species which have been there for centuries, taking advantage of habitats which may be subject to sudden man-made change but where the change follows a regular and predictable pattern. The species were not sown or put there by man. They are either relic features or they were able to colonize the sites at a time when the surrounding land was a lot less inhospitable than it is today. The intensification of agriculture and the scale of urban development have combined to isolate species within these relic sites, allowing little or no genetic exchange between them. This inevitably raises concerns about the long-term evolution and survival of species.

MALHAM TARN, YORKSHIRE DALES NATIONAL PARK

This early morning photograph shows a clump of broad buckler fern growing in a wet, boggy woodland.

Species which have become isolated and fail to take advantage of new opportunities can be regarded as indicators of either ancient habitats or a long continuity of consistent management. The occurrence of a single species is not significant but, when several such species occur together, important conclusions can be drawn. The concentration of rare arctic–alpine plants in Upper Teesdale, for example, strongly suggests an exceptionally long period without tree cover. The rich lichen flora on old trees in the New Forest is evidence that mature trees have been present there continuously for an exceptionally long period. An abundance of small-leaved lime strongly suggests ancient woodland and any doubts are soon dismissed when it is accompanied by a rich ground flora. On downland, an intimate mixture of many plants, such as chalk milkwort, horseshoe vetch, burnt orchid and bastard toadflax, suggests a long history of grazing without ploughing or fertilizer.

It is very important to maintain such species in their traditional setting. Moving species and tending them in a semi-natural environment cuts them off from the history which created and shaped the habitat. Such action is akin to preserving a vintage car without its engine! Conservation organizations need to subsidize or emulate past management practices to ensure that habitats survive in a manner compatible with their origins. This should help to perpetuate populations of both typical communities and rare and declining species. There are also great educational benefits in helping to demonstrate the origins of our wildlife heritage.

Maintaining long-established habitats and species with poor powers of dispersal and colonization is an obvious priority for conservationists. We must protect the irreplaceable vastness of the flow country of northern Scotland, though few of us may ever see it. The conservation of the massive oak pollards of Windsor Forest with their attendant rare beetles also merits high priority because many of the beetles are unknown elsewhere. Such features cannot be replaced but the aim of nature conservation is primarily to maintain a diversity of wildlife so that it can be enjoyed by the public. Aesthetics and public opinion must be brought into the balance; everyone is entitled to their own viewpoint. Who is to say whether it is more important to maintain populations of goldfinches in field margins or to protect the last county locality of a rare moss or millipede? Both are important but public support relies on concern, comprehension and motivation. To maintain this, people must be able to appreciate wildlife without a great investment in time and trouble. A widespread scatter of interesting nature reserves and other protected areas is essential and we must not forget the city dweller, who has every right to commune with nature in green oases among the concrete. An interest in wildlife, developed at an early age in an urban environment, may grow into a lifelong passion.

Where should conservation go from here? There will always be more to strive for, competing pressures and new trends raising novel difficulties or opportunities. The cornerstone of nature conservation, which is to safeguard the most important wildlife sites, remains unchanged and experience has shown that ownership by a conservation body is the best assurance of long-term viability. Achievements in this area can be warmly applauded. Past governments have supported the purchase of prime sites and the Nature Conservancy Council now manages no fewer than 220 national nature reserves. The Royal Society for the Protection of Birds and the National Trust both own magnificent suites of reserves including much of Britain's most attractive and scientifically interesting countryside, and local authorities manage over 150 statutory Local Nature Reserves, all of which are readily available for enjoyment by local people and school-children.

These are fine achievements but they are fully matched by the work of the County Wildlife Trusts. These have grown steadily in number, stature and influence, providing a continuous record of achievement which, happily, is still snowballing. The movement began to gather momentum fifty years after the formation of the body which later became the Royal Society for Nature Conservation, the umbrella body to the Wildlife Trusts.

Membership and income of the Wildlife Trusts is still increasing but not as rapidly as their problems, pressures and demands. Hard-pressed professionals guide the efforts of armies of volunteers, who willingly devote much of their energy, imagination, time and indeed money to nature conservation projects within their local areas. The Trusts now manage approximately 1800 nature reserves covering nearly 52,000 hectares (128,000 acres) and encompassing the full range of wildlife habitats and communities. Their efforts seem particularly worthwhile because they involve such a large number of people and their activities reflect one of the underlying objectives of the whole movement, that is, the appreciation and enjoyment of wildlife by the general public.

Despite the striking achievements of the conservation bodies, depressing losses of habitat and associated wildlife still continue. The blackest period was probably the twenty years after the last war, when economic factors and government initiatives produced massive improvements in agricultural output, plantation forestry on a scale never seen before and urban development, with scarcely a thought for any life other than human. Since the 1940s there has been a loss of about 45% of Britain's ancient semi-natural woodland, 40% of lowland heathland and no less than 95% of lowland, herb-rich grassland. At least 225,000 km (140,000 miles) of hedgerow have been destroyed since 1950 and, if this is not bad enough, most of the remainder is mechanically trimmed into an unobtrusive, flat-topped rectangle which cannot get in the way of farming and is of little use to the many species which are known to use hedges. Farming has adopted the techniques of the production line and wildlife has been the loser.

Today many of the pressures and trends are changing but threats and damage are still with us. In upland Britain, mass afforestation is the matter of gravest concern, with

GANNET COLONY

G*rassholme Island, off the Pembrokeshire coast, becomes almost white in spring when the gannets arrive to breed. The colony contains several thousand breeding pairs.*

Overleaf

HIGHLAND LOCH

I*n the evening sun, the tops of bogbeans poke their heads through the still, serene waters of a small loch near Loch Broom, Perthshire.*

long-established, semi-natural habitats containing internationally important bird populations being replaced by a monotonous blanket of alien conifers. Heather moorland is changing into grassland because the agricultural support system favours overstocking rather than subsidizing the level of grazing which the land will support. In the lowlands, heathlands continue to change into birch woodland because the grazing which maintained them in the past is no longer economic. The pace of commercial development in south-eastern England is putting unprecedented pressure on semi-natural grasslands, heathlands and wetlands, and the last surviving herb-rich meadows in private ownership are always in danger because they depend on a traditional form of uneconomic management which has probably been practised for several decades by die-hard owner/occupiers who were prepared to turn their backs on agricultural advice and grants. The condition of our rivers and coastal waters has deteriorated because any improvement in sewage effluent and other polluting discharges can only be achieved by a huge investment which the government seems loath to support or demand.

There is a great need for more nature reserves but most require a level of management which voluntary conservation bodies find difficult to support. Money is required not only for land purchase but also for running expenses. For example, meadows must be safeguarded by grazing or cutting for hay if their essential character is to be maintained, and the grazing of chalk downland must be properly planned and supervised if the decline of jewels like the silver-spotted skipper and the adonis blue butterflies is to be reversed. There is scope too for

reversing over-zealous land drainage in some low-lying grasslands to encourage the return of nesting snipe, redshank and curlew. Coastal areas need stringent protection if they are to survive the twin pressures of development and recreation. The breeding colonies of terns, cliff-nesting seabirds and seals are of paramount importance. Vigilance and determination will be required in good measure if they are to be protected from over-fishing and pollution.

Other species can only be brought back from the brink of extinction by adjustments in farming and forestry. In the uplands, we must ensure that no more of the open ground required by golden plover, greenshank, peregrine and golden eagle is lost to forestry. Populations of the beleaguered merlin and red kite could increase if only there was a larger area of suitable habitat for hunting. In lowland farmland, agricultural over-production has given us the opportunity to provide the habitat required by the barn owl and stone curlew. Otters could make a comeback if more rivers were protected from pollution and habitat destruction. Above all, we must ensure that no avoidable extinctions are allowed to occur. We may be too late for the red-backed shrike but we must not lose others like the chough, bittern, sand lizard, natterjack toad or monkey orchid. The ultimate obstacle to realizing such objectives is often ignorance or lack of will on the part of too many people. I hope this book will play at least a small part in overcoming these obstacles.

Julian Pettifer

THE COAST
introduction by Hammond Innes

'*I never thought mud could be so beautiful.*' My wife Dorothy said that the first time we moored below Shotley, just inside the Orwell River, and woke to the piping of curlews right alongside, probing the mud with their curved beaks. The East Anglian coast is mostly flat with long fingers of water running deep inland, the estuaries fringed with broad expanses of mud at low tide, and beyond the mud, the saltings or the flat of reclaimed fenland.

That bulging bit of England is the most water-orientated part of our coast. While the legions marched the Roman roads, their baggage and the supplies for fort and town went by barge. Later those same waterways were used by the marauding peoples of the Scandinavian Viks, who finally settled and gave their family names to many of the villages and hamlets.

There are two ways of looking at a coastline, from the land or from the sea. From the sea our country divides roughly on a line Dover to Cape Wrath, most of our western coast being rock and cliff, the eastern half low-lying, almost awash with the polluted waters of the North Sea. This latter is a coast that is mostly sinking, the line of it constantly shifting, shingle, sand and mud bank slowly moving south, high tides, combined with periodic surges, pounding at the sea defences, inundating the flat lands behind. Given a decade or two of melting north polar seas, due to the 'greenhouse effect' of man's pollution, and all these low-lying areas, including half of London, will be under water.

The south coast mirrors the French shore, evidence of the break-in of the Atlantic, the chalk downs of Kent and Sussex giving way to sandstone and then to Devonian formations, and finally, at Land's End, you move much further back in time to the pre-Cambrian granitic outcrop that is a magma relic of very ancient volcanic activity. From then on, all the way up the western coast, it is largely volcanic, the whole cliff line of the English, Welsh and Scottish shore, testimony to the violence of that igneous activity.

Something that has always amused me is the reaction of the sailor to the differing coasts. I learned my sailing, and my navigation, in the North Sea and on the Thames banks, and I was dead scared when I first went west down-Channel to face a coast of solid rock. I never revealed this to anyone until I discovered that far better sailors than I, brought up in the West Country, were equally scared coming east, where all the coastal hazards are under water and the tidal streams between the hidden banks totally unpredictable.

The wildlife and plants in both areas are vastly different, the migrant geese, the avocets and the saltmarsh flora in the east, the preponderance of seabirds, gannets and cliff flowers in the west. This is, of course, a reflection of the very unusual climatic conditions, the geographical position of our islands.

Go from the Clyde out through the Kyles of Bute and up Loch Fyne to Crinan by way of the canal of that name, and there, right in front of you, is Scarba and the Gate to the Isles, with the terrible tidal race of the Corryvreckan on your port hand. This was the coast that gave Gavin Maxwell his chapter title: 'There Be Dragons'. The 'monsters' follow the food supply and this is a coast that teems with life – porpoise and basking shark, fish and seabird, gannets diving, shearwaters skimming and guillemots by the acre.

Sailing south through the Firth of Lorn by Colonsay and Islay the sea seems alive with fish, whale and seabird. Then, as you approach the Irish coast suddenly it goes dead, or it did when I was spinnakering down that coast, and it continued so almost as far south as the Blaskets. Going north to Orkney and Shetland, on the other hand, the sea remains full of life. I went all over the Shetland Islands when I was researching *North Star* and waiting to go out to live for a time on one of the North Sea rigs, but alas, I never saw the snowy owl and a little girl told me 'the doigs had flug'd.' That was in the early days when Sullom Voe, that almost land-locked stretch of water, was still unspoilt. Now it is a collecting point for North Sea oil, and an additional hazard for all the wildlife of this remote area.

Over-fishing and oil pollution, these are the threats that man poses to the wildlife habitat of our northern coasts. However spectacular the scenery, when the birds and the seals are gone, it will never be the same again. But in all my travels I have never found any area of the world to equal the British Isles for the variety of the coastal scenery.

MULLION COVE, CORNWALL

*H*airy greenweed and kidney vetch light up the cliff-tops.

The changing shoreline

The subject of this chapter is the narrow strip of land which, when it is drawn on a map, provides the outline of Great Britain, including its islands. The landward limit of the strip is the line beyond which salt spray ceases to influence wildlife and the other edge can be taken as low water spring tides, the vertical height below which the sea never drops. Within this coastal strip there is a remarkable range of habitats and a very large number of plant and animal species. Indeed, Great Britain could claim to have the most varied coastline of any country in the world.

Coastal habitats are created, moulded and controlled largely by the physical power of the sea. Tides and currents are constantly at work but every now and again the turmoil of air movement, which creates our weather, throws up high winds and storms. These can generate huge waves and send them crashing towards the edge of the land with awesome destructive force. Vast quantities of material are carried off by seething waves but the laws of physics dictate that most of it will not be carried too far.

The sea is constantly at work reshaping the coast, eroding the land in one place and depositing material in another. These processes create a range of habitats, depending on local geology and the shape of the coastline. The degree of exposure to the prevailing westerly winds is an important factor in determining which species can survive. Aspect and shelter affect the distance

SHELL SAND IN THE MORAY FIRTH

A natural mixture of shells amongst the sand by the dunes at Nairn on the Moray Firth, east Scotland. Many of the sandy beaches of this part of Scotland have masses of shells washed up on them, of numerous different species. These were photographed just as they occurred, without any rearrangement.

reached by storm waves and sea spray. Many species, especially trees, are intolerant of high winds and direct exposure to salt water but they can flourish where there is adequate physical protection, such as in some Scottish sea lochs and sheltered creeks like the deep, steep-sided estuaries of south Devon and Cornwall.

Estuaries and mudflats

Vast amounts of material eroded by the sea are carried until the water is calm enough to allow it to fall. This is most likely to happen in sheltered bays. Here the material is evenly deposited on each tide, very gradually raising the level and extending the area of intertidal mud. Such flats may have a profile very close to horizontal and the width of foreshore at low tide can stretch further than the eye can see, such as on the coasts of Essex and Lancashire, and in the Wash. Soft sediments are too mobile to permit the growth of rooted plants but as the mud stabilizes, green algae such as sea lettuce may be established. The certainty of the tidal cycle has permitted the evolution of a diverse community of invertebrates, with species from many disparate groups, the larger animals being mainly segmented worms and bivalve molluscs such as cockles. These are often present at a high density, providing a vital food supply for enormous numbers of birds.

The daily supply of plankton brought by the tide and the regular deposition of fresh sediment provides all the food for the invertebrates concealed in the mud.

Ecologists have calculated that intertidal mudflats produce more living matter per unit area than any terrestrial habitat. This high productivity is even further enhanced in estuaries. Here the twice-daily ingress of salt water is met by a steady seaward passage of fresh water which brings with it huge quantities of minerals, nutrients and organic matter. Many invertebrates are adapted to the reduction of salinity found in estuaries, and the species naturally arrange themselves on a gradient from nearly fresh water to full-strength seawater. The total numbers of invertebrates are greatly elevated in estuaries, so that the food resource available to birds is formidable.

Britain's estuaries have great international importance as winter feeding grounds for waders and wildfowl, particularly those breeding in northern and western Europe, Siberia, Iceland and Greenland. Our coastline is particularly well endowed with large estuaries which remain free of ice and where birds can feed during low tide, relatively untroubled by human disturbance. The total British wintering population of waders is well in excess of a million birds, and counts of over 100,000 are regular events at major sites such as the Wash, the Ribble estuary and Morecambe Bay. Several estuaries have winter wader populations not far short of this, notably the Thames, Dee, Humber, Solway, Severn, Forth, Strangford Lough and Chichester and Langstone Harbours.

Some wader and waterfowl species are thinly spread round all Britain's estuaries whereas others, in particular dunlin and knot, stay together in huge flocks and favour a relatively small number of major sites. All these birds have one essential requirement – a place where they can all roost safely together when the feeding ground is covered by the tide.

When an area of mudflats has been raised to a certain level it will be colonized by glasswort, an upright, succulent green plant. For centuries people on the East Anglian coast have collected glasswort for sale or home consumption as 'samphire', serving it in the same way that one would serve asparagus.

As the mudflats rise, other species are able to colonize the more stable surface and, by arresting the movement of the water, the vegetation itself accelerates deposition of further silt. This habitat, known as saltmarsh, contains a wide range of specialist, salt-tolerant plants (halophytes), demonstrating interesting zonation from the lower limit to the upper reaches which are only flooded by spring tides. One of the most distinctive and attractive of the saltmarsh plants is sea lavender, which can create a shimmering purple haze in late summer.

Rocky coasts

Many large mudflats contain a high proportion of sand laid down by more rapidly moving water. Sandy beaches are deposited by the tide, the material sometimes having been picked up by turbulent currents offshore. Such beaches are so unstable that very little plant or animal life can be sustained in the sand. Where mud or rocks occur, the situation changes dramatically. Rocky foreshores are among the most interesting of all coastal habitats, supporting an attractive array of plants and animals very different in character from those in habitats inland. The plants are all algae rather than higher plants, and they come in a range of forms and colours. They are classified into brown, red and blue/green, and between them they help to create the conditions needed for a spectacular array of seashore animals. Investigating rock pools during summer seaside holidays has exerted an early influence on many a famous naturalist. These beautiful pools do not stay tranquil for long, however, and all the animals must have the ability to cling on or find suitable crannies where they can shelter from crashing waves.

The most interesting stretches of rocky foreshore are generally along the western seaboard, where the hardest rocks occur, but one notable exception is Robin Hood's Bay in Yorkshire, where the Jurassic limestone meets the North Sea. There are many miles of interesting rocky coastline in Cornwall, Pembrokeshire, western Scotland and Northern Ireland, and the Channel Isles, Scillies and Lundy support disproportionate numbers of rare species.

Blue-rayed limpets at low water, south Wales.

Sand dunes

On many stretches of coast, each high tide brings a fresh supply of sand, gradually raising the upper part of the foreshore. Once sun and wind have dried out the surface, the sand particles can be picked up and blown, either along the beach or inland. Most of them come to rest when their progress is interrupted by an object slowing the wind at ground level. That object could be strandline flotsam but it could also be a plant capable of growing in mobile sand. One such species is marram, the familiar, tall, wiry grass which forms distinct arching tussocks in coastal sand dunes. The form of the plant is well adapted for catching wind-blown sand which accumulates around its base. As the sand rises, the plant can extend its rhizomes almost indefinitely, sending up new leaves and spikes of fluffy inflorescences. The process continues until the height of the dunes ensures that the rate of erosion exceeds the rate of

Brown hare tracks amongst the sand dunes.

accumulation. For dunes to become very large there needs to be an adequate supply of sand replenishing the beach and not too many humans to accelerate the natural process of erosion. What often happens is that, once a dune ridge has developed, another one starts to form on its seaward side. Over time, large dune systems may develop, consisting of a series of ridges running parallel to the shore.

Sand dunes are a very rich habitat with a great many characteristic plants and insects. It is essentially a natural ecosystem in which man's influence may be minimal, though most British dune systems are now affected by too many human feet and by a few invasive plant species unwisely introduced from other countries. The younger dunes support such attractive plants as sea rocket, sea sandwort, yellow horned-poppy, sea bindweed, sea spurge and sea holly. Older dunes may support a wide range of species and the community will be strongly influenced by the amount of calcium in the sand derived from fragments of shells.

The hollows between dune ridges are often permanently wet, receiving the rainwater which has percolated through the dune sand. The plant communities of these dune slacks range from those resembling wet heath, with *Sphagnum* mosses and cross-leaved heath, to calcareous rich fen with several sedges, brooklime and marsh orchids.

Shingle coasts

Shingle ridges, such as Chesil Beach, Hurst Spit and Orford Ness, are formed in a more violent way than sand dunes. The pebbles are a great deal bigger than sand particles and the force required to throw them up into a ridge is a great deal stronger. They are thrown up and added to by storms, but between these events they are pretty static.

Only specially adapted species can withstand the harsh conditions offered by shingle. Daytime temperatures can be very high in summer and the freely draining shingle can become totally dehydrated. The plants must not only be able to reduce or eliminate water loss but also be capable of taking advantage of the condensation which forms on cool pebbles towards dawn. Typical shingle plants include yellow horned-poppy and the enormous, cabbage-like sea-kale. Shingle in the northern parts of Britain may support the distinctive grey foliage of the oysterplant.

The largest shingle system in Britain is at Dungeness in south-east Kent. This is an amazing system of parallel ridges and slacks. The flora is extremely rich and the oldest ridges carry dense holly scrub. The longest shingle ridge in Europe is the 24-kilometre sweep of Chesil Beach to the west of Portland in Dorset. This enormous ridge, maintained by westerly gales which have neatly arranged the pebbles in a gradient of decreasing size, from west to east, separates the sea from the beautiful brackish lagoon known as the Fleet.

Another very distinctive habitat and one better represented in Britain than anywhere else in the world is the machair of the Western Isles of Scotland and coast of Donegal. This is a low, undulating, grassy landscape which in early summer is a mass of flowers. The dominant influences are the very strong, salt-laden, westerly winds and violent winter storms. The wind provides a supply of calcareous shell sand but it is too strong to allow dune formation. The turf is grazed by geese in winter and in most cases by sheep.

The main summer inhabitants of the flower-studded turf, however, are waders, particularly ringed plover, dunlin, oystercatcher and redshank, which all nest at exceptionally high densities. Wheatear, corn bunting and twite are also common breeding birds of this habitat.

Cliffs

The variety and beauty of rocky shores around Britain should be the envy of the world. Few people can be unimpressed by the stark white cliffs of Dover, the soft, slumping undercliffs of parts of Dorset and the Isle of Wight, the flowery limestone and sandstone headlands of south-west England and Pembrokeshire, the dark, basalt cliffs of County Antrim and the massive granite and sandstone crags falling vertically several hundred metres for miles around Scotland and the Western Isles.

Cliffs are formed by waves undermining the base of a land mass, causing it to fall into the sea. The rock type and its structure determine how rapidly the cliff-face erodes, the angle of the cliff-face, the size of the chunks which fall, whether soil or organic matter is able to accumulate, and the character of any vegetation. The geology of Britain is highly varied and the same is true of our cliffs. The more gently sloping surfaces support a greater range of vegetation because it is easier for soil to develop and for plants to get a toehold. The longer a cliff remains stable between rockfalls, the greater the diversity of vegetation, but the sequence is usually interrupted before scrub can be established and grow into woodland.

The limestone and sandstone cliffs of Devon, Cornwall and south Wales are particularly attractive, with many colourful flowers such as thyme, spring squill and sheep's-bit. Where soil has been allowed to settle, taller plants such as alexanders, fennel and tree mallow form a distinctive habitat. The clifftops of the Channel Isles and the Lizard peninsula in south Cornwall are a botanist's paradise, for here the mild climate and the peculiar local geology have permitted the survival of a staggering array of rare plants.

Seabirds

A mixed seabird colony of shags, guillemots and kittiwakes on the Farne Islands.

Other, harder cliffs are more noted for their seabird colonies. Narrow ledges on sheer cliffs offer sanctuary from persecution and predators, particularly on islands, and Britain's coast provides the nesting requirements of a high proportion of the seabirds of the northern Atlantic. There are so many huge and spectacular nesting colonies that it is not easy to single out the most magnificent. The RSPB has afforded protection to a good number of them, such as at South Stack in Anglesey, Rathlin Island in Antrim, Fowlsheugh in Grampian, Handa in Sutherland, Noup Cliffs, Marwick Head and Papa Westray in Orkney, St Bees Head in Cumbria and Bempton in Yorkshire.

Many of these reserves are also good places to watch seals. There are two British species, the common and the grey seal. Despite persecution, controlled culling, marine pollution and disease, both species are present in numbers large enough be considered a threat to the livelihood of fishermen. Britain has a clear international obligation to protect seal colonies, however, particularly for the grey seal, as nearly half its world population breeds in our coastal waters.

FLOCK OF BRENT GEESE, KEYHAVEN, HAMPSHIRE

*N*umbers of the dark-breasted race of the Brent geese, seen here, have increased enormously in recent years. They winter along the south and east coast of England and now feed mainly on grass leys rather than their traditional food, eel-grass. In some places special areas of grassland are being set aside for them, to reduce conflict with farmers.

Each seabird species has its ideal nest site so the available space is shared out in a predictable manner. The flat tops of rocky islets and grassy cliff slopes are favoured by gannets, herring gulls and the two black-backed gulls. The flat tops of low islands are also used by breeding colonies of terns. Rabbit burrows on these slopes may be used by puffins and Manx shearwaters. Cormorants and shags are likely to nest on the lower parts of broken rocky cliffs of no great height. Cormorants usually nest on their own but shags happily mix with other species. In Northern Ireland, north Wales and western Scotland, among the broken rocks at the foot of a cliff is where the black guillemot, or tystie, usually nests. Razorbills and guillemots favour taller, sheer cliffs, from which their young will have a clear drop to the sea below. They manage to use apparently insecure ledges by sticking their eggs to the bare rock with a covering of guano. Fulmars, those masters of the stiff-winged glide, have increased so that they now breed on nearly every sheer cliff-face more than about sixty metres high. They will use the narrowest of ledges and defend them vigorously against intruders by spitting an evil fluid. The very narrowest ledges on the tallest cliffs are where one should expect to see colonies of the kittiwake, easily recognized by the snow-white body and wingtips dipped in ink.

All colonial seabirds are very vulnerable to oil pollution, both near the breeding sites and also when they are feeding in concentrations out at sea. A great deal more is now known about the distribution of seabirds at sea throughout the year and liaison arrangements have greatly improved to reduce the impact of accidental pollution. Above all, however, seabirds are heavily dependent on healthy fish stocks in coastal waters.

LOCH SCRIDAIN, MULL

A beautiful view of the west coast sea-loch at low tide, where a stream enters the loch at Pennyghael. In the background is Ben More, Mull's highest mountain. Otters and many other animals and birds feed along these productive, undisturbed shores.

The impact of man

In the Western Isles and in many of the more remote parts of mainland Scotland, low coastlines exhibit perfectly natural transitions from intertidal to terrestrial conditions. Very few transitions of this sort can be found in England and Wales because the land has been intensively used for agriculture or other purposes and for generations man has been building walls to keep the sea at bay. Intensive drainage and fertilizer run-off from pasture and arable crops have led to a great reduction in the plant species associated with brackish water, such as soft hornwort and tasselweed, and plants and birds of semi-natural grassland influenced by salt spray.

Modern sea-walls are either massive concrete structures or wide, clay embankments. Given time the latter accumulate quite an interesting range of plants and varied insect populations. Weed seeds and insects on these banks

are a vital food resource for migrant birds moving along the coast or grounded by bad weather. In winter the seeds present in such habitats sustain flocks of birds from upland or Arctic habitats, notably snow buntings, Lapland buntings and shore larks.

Though the greater part of our coastline holds some interest for the observant naturalist, and some sections of coast can be considered very nearly natural, the overwhelming majority has been significantly affected by man. There are hundreds of kilometres of sea-walls and breakwaters, dating from the medieval period to the present. Groynes at right angles to the beach trap sand which would otherwise build up intertidal flats. The greater proportion of our soft cliffs has been protected by revetments or other sea-defence works to prevent them from crumbling into the sea. The pressure for such coastal engineering usually comes from the owners of properties which were built too close to the top of the cliff, and some acute conflicts can develop where constant scouring of the cliff-face is required to expose internationally important fossil beds or other geological features. So many kilometres of soft cliffs have been protected that the supply of sediments for mudflats and saltmarsh has been seriously depleted in many areas. These habitats are also being squeezed from the other direction by new sea-walls enclosing upper saltmarsh for grazing and subsequent arable agriculture.

Most of our larger estuaries and intertidal mudflats have been heavily used in the past for wildfowling, which obviously had a major influence on the numbers, movements and behaviour of waders, geese and other wildfowl. Fortunately, the understanding between wildfowlers and conservation interests is very good today, so that major roosts and feeding grounds are left largely undisturbed. The pressure from wildfowlers has to a large extent been replaced, however, by the ever-growing demands of the leisure boom. Birds are increasingly disturbed by water-skiing, windsurfing, sailing, powerboating, jet-skiing, parascending and whatever other activities our fertile imagination can dream up for shallow tidal water. The impact is not confined to disturbance, for there is also great pressure for barrages, marinas, quays and the dredging of new channels, all of which further reduce a declining and finite resource.

Even the wilder parts of the western coast of Scotland, which one might have thought were largely immune from man's commercialism, have been tainted – in this case by an explosion of marine fish farming. Any sheltered sea loch seems suitable for producing salmon, turbot, halibut and other fish on a large scale in submerged cages. The intertidal habitats are damaged by effluent and generally raised levels of nutrients, and more of the coastline is further affected by onshore developments, improved access and disturbance. The tragedy is that this was such a magnificent unspoilt area, formerly so lightly touched by the sparse resident population of crofters and lobster fishermen.

There is a great need to increase controls over fish farming to protect the best of the rugged, rocky coast with its wealth of flowers, seals, otters, eider ducks, peregrines and recently reintroduced sea eagles. The conflict between the fish farmers and those moved to protect the natural beauty of this coastline is very sharp and immediate. This contrasts with the more sinister but nevertheless severe impacts of pollution and over-fishing such as the decimation of the sand-eel shoals in north Scotland, where breeding seabird colonies have been hit disastrously in recent years. Surely the stakes are far too high to tolerate such selfish, short-term exploitation.

CLIFF FLOWERS, GUERNSEY

*P*art of the glorious display of flowers (opposite) that illuminates all the southern cliffs of Guernsey throughout the spring. Sea campion, gorse, and bluebells (a common cliff species in western Britain) are visible here, amongst other species, photographed in the evening near Moulin Huet.

GORSE ON THE GUERNSEY CLIFFS

*T*he lower rockier slopes of Guernsey's southern cliffs are often less flowery, but in places they light up with masses of the prostrate form of common gorse, shown here, or common broom. In these clumps, there are so many flowers that the foliage is barely visible! The photograph was taken near Les Corbières.

THE SEVEN SISTERS, SUSSEX

*T*he chalk cliffs east of
Cuckmere Haven in East
Sussex are a famous
landmark. They are also
notable for many downland
flowers on their tops, where
the strong maritime influence
dwarfs and changes the flora.
There are chalk cliffs on both
sides of the haven and, as
can be seen, the beach itself is
made up largely of fragments
of chalk together with flint
nodules dissolved from the
chalk. Much of the area is
managed as a Local Nature
Reserve by the county council.
The photograph was taken in
August and it is noticeable
how brown and dry the
downs look by late summer.

25

YELLOW HORNED POPPY ON SHINGLE

*T*his photograph (above) demonstrates how little vegetation survives on the seaward side of shingle banks, where the stones are constantly moving, there is no soil and there is heavy salt spray. This lone plant of yellow horned poppy was at Shingle Street, Suffolk, facing out across the North Sea.

SEA KALE, SHINGLE STREET

A superb clump of sea kale in full flower (opposite) at Shingle Street, Suffolk, with the coastguard cottages beyond and another clump of kale just visible. In many areas, the young shoots of kale were eaten as a vegetable (and occasionally still are). It was made more tender by mounding the shingle around each plant to blanch it.

SHINGLE STREET, SUFFOLK

*M*obile coastal shingle is an inhospitable habitat, and few plants can do well on it. The photograph shows a mixture of the beautiful sea pea with a large clump of sea kale beyond. These are two real shingle specialists, that rarely grow anywhere else.

LOW TIDE, LUNDY, DEVON

*T*he seas around the island of Lundy, at the western edge
of the Bristol Channel, are a statutory Marine Nature
Reserve. At very low tides, you can get a glimpse of the
richness of the marine life at the edge of the sea.

ROCKPOOL LIFE, INISHEER ARAN ISLES

*T*he western coasts of the British Isles support a remarkable array of life, much of which can be seen at low tide. This photograph (right) shows a beautiful multi-coloured rockpool on a limestone shore, full of plants and animals.

PUFFIN, HANDA ISLAND

A puffin steadies itself in strong westerly winds, which constantly affect its breeding grounds on the high western cliffs of Handa. They are one of our most attractive birds, with their distinctive beak and engaging habits. Though still common in places, they have declined considerably in some areas.

INTERTIDAL LIFE, WEST SCOTLAND

A close view of some of the intertidal life to be found in the clear sheltered waters of west Scotland's sea-lochs. Almost every stone has something growing on it and the life underneath the stones is even more varied.

SEABIRD COLONIES, HANDA ISLAND

Off the far north-west of Scotland lies the island of Handa, a reserve run by the Royal Society for the Protection of Birds. The seabird colonies around its western cliffs are spectacular, with tens of thousands of guillemots, razorbills, fulmars, puffins and other species constantly coming and going.

LOCH TORRIDON AT LOW TIDE

The west coast of Scotland has a massive number of sea-lochs, drowned valleys that have many of the characteristics of lochs, but are actually part of the sea. Their extra shelter compared with exposed coasts usually means that there is a marvellous array of intertidal plants and animals, with a dense growth of seaweeds. The abundant food supply and their undisturbed nature, attracts creatures, like otters, herons and hooded crows, to feed along the shoreline at low tide. This view shows Loch Torridon, in Ross and Cromarty, looking north across the loch from a bay called Camas a Chlarsair to the massive bulk of Ben Alligin. The amount of algal growth can readily be seen in the foreground and middle distance.

SEA SPURGE, BRAUNTON BURROWS, DEVON

*T*he strange-looking plants of sea spurge (above) can grow in inhospitable places, on bare sand dunes, where little else survives. These superb high dunes are part of the massive system at Braunton Burrows in Devon, much of which lies within a National Nature reserve.

COMMON SEALS, NORTH NORFOLK

A mass of common seals basking on the sandbanks off Blakeney, on the north Norfolk coast. Although their numbers have been badly hit by disease recently, this area, and the Wash, is still a marvellous place to see this species. This group consists mainly of adults, with a few young amongst them.

GOLDEN SAMPHIRE, HURST LIGHTHOUSE

The end of the long shingle spit at Hurst Castle, Hampshire, is an intriguing blend of shingle and saltmarsh. There are wonderful displays of golden samphire, visible here in late summer, and other flowers at different times. The whole area is managed as a Local Nature Reserve by the County Council.

CLIFF-TOP FLOWERS, THE LIZARD, CORNWALL

A superb display of cliff-top flowers on a headland on the east side of The Lizard, photographed at dawn in mid-May as the sun's rays just light up the flowers. The main clump is sea-campion, with thrift, and smaller amounts of bluebells and other species visible.

MULTI-COLOURED CLIFF FLOWERS, CORNWALL

A lovely mixture of May cliff-top flowers at Mullion Cove in Cornwall. The blue is spring squill, a relative of the bluebell; the pink flowers are thrift, or sea-pink; and the yellow is kidney vetch. The mass of flowers can be so great as to cover huge areas of cliff with colour for a short time in late spring.

CLIFF-TOP SPLENDOUR, THE LIZARD

A spectacular grouping of gorse, sea campion and bluebell.

BEETLE ON CREEPING WILLOW

*T*he striking red colour of the poplar leaf beetle (left) shows up clearly on the mass of creeping willow on which it feeds. (Poplars and willows are closely related and the beetle feeds on both.) This willow is flourishing in a dune slack at Braunton Burrows, Devon, and the white patch is its mass of fluffy seeds.

MATING PUSS MOTHS

A pair of mating puss moths still visible out in the open just after dawn, though later in the day they will probably move under cover. They are sitting on a spike of sea rush, on the dunes at Braunton Burrows, Devon, which is a National Nature Reserve.

MARSH ORCHIDS, LINCOLNSHIRE COAST

*P*art of the fabulous display of marsh and spotted orchids
*(in a poor year!) at Saltfleetby, on the Lincolnshire coast.
The National Nature Reserve here is a lovely mixture of sand
dunes and grassland, with many wet areas.*

SEA STOCK, ISLE OF WIGHT

*T*he beautiful southern chalk cliffs of the Isle of Wight are
home to a number of uncommon plants, including the
lovely sea stock shown here. This is a rare species, just
occurring on a few southerly coastal sites, where it is probably
native. Here it grows right on the edge of the high cliffs.

THE ISLE OF PURBECK,
DORSET

*A*dramatic view along the
southern limestone cliffs
and slopes of the Isle of
Purbeck, Dorset. The
photograph was taken on a
bright windy April day, with
the dwarfed blackthorn
flowering profusely in the sun
and hugging the rocks to
escape the prevailing wind.

LOCH SCRIDAIN, MULL

*L*och Scridain is a sea loch on the west side of the island of Mull, off the west coast of Scotland. The photograph, taken late on a September evening, shows the state of the loch at the highest tide of the year and with a strong westerly wind pushing it higher still. At times like this, all the marginal vegetation becomes inundated and roads are often covered.

SHELL BEACH, ARAN ISLES

*D*iscarded sea-urchins, probably eaten by young otters, on an incredible beach made up entirely of shell fragments at Inisheer, in the Aran Isles. Young otters will feed on almost anything on the tideline, including many unproductive species like urchins and crabs.

OTTER FEEDING AT LOW TIDE

A young otter feeding on the shore of a sea-loch at very low tide in September. Otters regularly feed along the shoreline throughout western Scotland, both on the mainland and on the islands. Adults feed mainly at night, though young ones like this often feed throughout the day.

SPRING COAST
FLOWERS, GUERNSEY

*T*he coast of Guernsey
lights up with flowers
from March onwards
through into the summer.
This display of flowers, close
to Fort Hommet on the west
coast, shows dwarfed
common gorse and thrift in
flower together on a bright,
windy April day. Most of the
coast of Guernsey is unspoilt
and uncultivated, and there
are many uncommon flowers
here, as well as the superb
displays of common species.

45

WOODLANDS
introduction by Chris Baines

'*I love the way woodlands have always embraced me, welcomed me, and filled me with a sense of optimism. I suppose it's partly because they're a constant reminder of 'life out of death'. Woodlands are so full of vigour, and yet there's always the smell of decaying leaves and rotting wood, to complement the springtime perfume of bluebells, or the fruity smells of autumn.*'

Nothing else offers such a powerful celebration of the changing seasons either, and that is such a fundamental feature of the British landscape. At one time I worked in the endless summer of the Middle East, and I would always rush to woodland on my return, to soak up the sense of the seasons again.

As a child, growing up on the edge of Sheffield, I had most of my early adventures in the young woodlands that had sprung up amongst the ruins of faded industry, and although I never thought about it at the time, those leafy landscapes have shaped my later life. My familiarity with birch and sycamore saplings bursting out of cracks in derelict factory walls, and the swampy willow and alder woodland that had colonised the silted ponds of the tumbledown watermills were such a powerful demonstration of nature fighting back – healing the wounds of man. These were very much woodlands filled with friendly ghosts, places with a powerful human history – and that is an aspect of the landscape that thrills me constantly.

Wet woodlands are particularly rich in wildlife – the sound of springtime songbirds, many of them freshly landed from South Africa is always breathtaking. Spectacular as these vigorous young woodlands are though, they are nowhere near as rich as the mossy, musty tangle of truly ancient woodland. Here too, there is the constant presence of the friendly ghosts – generations of local people who have known the comforting shelter of old trees. Ancient woodlands are extra special – an immensely complex, and almost infinite network of interconnections between wild plants and animals; between life and death; between the past, the present and the future. There is no better way of getting close to the earth, of feeling its primeval heartbeat, than to bury yourself in the mouldy leafiness of an old woodland, with your hands in the earth, and your eyes looking up into the treetops. It's hard to understand why we still sacrifice these magical, irreplaceable places just to hide roads, plant cash-crop conifers, 'screening' industrial estates, or grow more un-needed crops.

In my lifetime, urban dereliction and shrinkage of the railways have created a great deal of new 'opportunist' woodland, but in that same post-war period, half the ancient woodlands that had survived 8000 years since the last ice age have been destroyed forever. Now, at last, we are waking up to their importance, not just as wildlife habitat, not just as nice places to visit, but as a fundamental key to the survival of the planet. We have an urgent need to breathe new life into our ailing woodlands, so that they in turn can breathe new life into us.

Chris Baines

ULLSWATER, LAKE DISTRICT

The mossy, green, humid interior of a woodland on the shores of Ullswater.

Wood pasture and coppice

Five thousand years ago mainland Britain was one vast forest. The only open areas were wetlands, mountains, exposed coastal areas and patches of ground much favoured by deer, boar, brown bear and wild cattle. The extent of open ground at this time is a hotly debated issue among ecologists for it must have been from such places that all our indigenous non-woodland plants and animals subsequently spread to colonize most of the land surface. It is clear that most of the land supported a blanket of deciduous woodland, normally referred to as the 'wildwood'. Whereas today's lowland landscape has a scatter of wooded islands in a sea of farmland, the wildwood is presumed to have had a scatter of open patches in a sea of trees.

The transformation of the landscape began when man started to fell and burn woodland to make way for crops and domesticated animals. The first major phase of woodland clearance took place in the Neolithic period, but the pace accelerated rapidly during the Iron Age with the manufacture of more efficient tools and a great demand for charcoal. The Anglo-Saxons later embarked on a further orgy of destruction until, by the time the Normans arrived, the distribution and pattern of woodland had become pretty stable. Even in upland areas, the great majority of the wildwood had been cleared and regeneration was prevented by grazing and burning. Most of the surviving areas of woodland were on very poor soils, on steep slopes and in the most inaccessible regions.

As the rate of clearance slowed in the lowlands, so the remaining patches of woodland came to be perceived as areas to be exploited. They became

WOODPILE, BRADFIELD WOODS, SUFFOLK

These incredible woods have been coppiced and managed for woodland produce since medieval times. The practice continues to this day.

Female pied flycatcher at her nest hole. These are typical birds of western sessile oak woods.

increasingly valued as a resource to support domestic stock and as a renewable supply of fuel, timber and poles. Man had learned to manage that most useful characteristic of deciduous trees and shrubs – the capacity to shoot again from the base after being cut down. All that was required to produce another crop from felled woodland was to prevent the fresh shoots from being eaten by the stock. Gradually two types of management arose: some woods were grazed while others were fenced to exclude animals and were cut to the ground at frequent intervals. These are known as wood pasture and coppice respectively, and the two systems have had a profound influence on our woodland plants and animals. Throughout historic times woodland has been too valuable to ignore; every scrap, with the exception only of a few of the most inaccessible sites in deep valleys or on steep hillsides, has come to be managed as either wood pasture or coppice. In late medieval times in southern England a practice developed of allowing stock to graze within the coppices during the last few years of the coppice cycle when the shoots were no longer susceptible to browsing. In general, however, we can regard ancient woodland as having been either grazed or coppiced, and the ecological factors within each are quite distinct.

In wood pasture the trees could be put to good use, and their lives extended, by pollarding. Branches were removed at a height of two to three metres so that the animals could not reach the young shoots. The cut material provided fuel and the leaves were fed to the animals. Between the pollards conditions were open and grassy, for tree and shrub seedlings were eaten as soon as they appeared. Woodland herbs would have suffered likewise from repeatedly losing most of their above-ground parts. The habitat was dominated by relatively small numbers of large, old trees.

In coppices, by contrast, there were no old trees. They were never allowed to get very big because they would have been too difficult to move and cut up, and they would also have slowed the growth of the more valued commodity, the coppice poles. In the absence of grazing stock, ground flora plants thrived in coppices and there would have been a profusion of flowers through spring and summer. The ecosystem was subject to sudden changes in conditions, from dense shade to total exposure to sun and wind, but many plants cope with this very well. They survive the unfavourable period as buried seeds, bulbs or rhizomes, and woodland insects and birds are able to move from one patch to another as it comes into appropriate condition.

The result of several centuries of continuous management was that wood pasture sites became havens for insects associated with mature trees and dead wood, as well as bark-living lichens, mosses and liverworts. Coppice, on the other hand, offered little scope for these groups but supported a multitude of flowering plants and insects associated with the shrub and herb layer.

With the abandonment of traditional woodland management over the last century, the visual distinction between coppice and wood pasture has become blurred. New generations of trees and shrubs have appeared between the old trees in wood pasture relics. In neglected coppices the trees have become larger and the understorey has been allowed to develop into a canopy. Clues to the history of a site are often provided by earthworks and the form of the oldest trees but a great deal is also revealed by the general mix of flora and fauna. If a site is rich in lichens it was in all probability a piece of wood pasture; and a site with a rich ground flora is likely to have been coppice.

The range of ground flora species is controlled by several factors such as geology, soils, drainage, dominant tree species, deer browsing and past management. If the ground flora consists of only one or two species over a large area, it suggests either a relatively young wood or a long period without management. Bluebell and dog's mercury can both become very dominant in shady, neglected woodland. When a lowland English wood has been actively managed over many years, these species are likely to be accompanied by primrose, wood anemone, sanicle, sweet woodruff, wood spurge, dog-violet and early purple orchid.

Scottish woodlands

In the Highlands of Scotland the range of deciduous trees and shrubs is restricted by climatic conditions. On the western seaboard there are some magnificent oak-woods dripping with luxuriant lichens and mosses, and birch grows well on some open hillsides but many trees and other woodland plants are absent or very restricted in Scotland. The climate is too severe for many species and others have failed to survive the centuries of burning and grazing. Scots pine, however, is well adapted to both climate and soils and quite extensive areas of native pinewood have managed to survive in the Highlands as wood pasture. It has been driven to extinction, however, by the intensity of coppice management which has prevailed for so long in the lowlands. Like all conifers, it fails to regrow if cut off below the first whorl of leaves. All the Scots pine present today in England and Wales is the result of subsequent replanting by man.

In the Highlands, however, more than 10,000 hectares (24,500 acres) of native pinewood still survives, forming a distinctive habitat which has probably changed little in recent centuries. Birch is usually present and there may be an understorey of juniper over a carpet of heather, bilberry and cowberry. Many of the pinewoods such as Abernethy, Rothiemurchus and Glen Tanar have a very attractive, open character, with heavily branched trees and natural open clearings. In this delightful habitat a large number of relict insects have not only survived but have colonized new conifer plantations. Conifers were first planted in Scotland in the eighteenth century but their extent has increased dramatically in recent decades. These man-made forests are never likely to develop the character of the native pinewoods.

Old trees and dead wood

Silver-washed fritillary feeding on bramble beside a woodland ride.

'What is a healthy tree?' A forester might say 'a tall, sound, well-formed, rapidly growing specimen with no signs of fungal or other infections'. An alternative viewpoint is 'any tree whose appearance suggests that it is likely to live for a very long time'. Such a tree may have broken and dead limbs, dead wood in all stages of decay and disintegration through the actions of fungi and insects, and may have a totally hollow stem. The inner part of the bole of an old tree is of no functional significance other than adding a bit of mechanical strength. When an old tree has shed most of its large limbs, it no longer requires that strength to stay upright, and it will be better able to do so if it can reduce its weight. Loss of the inner bole is a perfectly natural stage in the ageing process of a healthy tree.

Our native trees are capable of living in harmony with a host of apparent agents of destruction. A good example of this is a small moth called the green

BEECH WOOD, NEW FOREST

The extraordinary 'ancient and ornamental' woods of this area may be poor for flowers, but they are exceptionally rich in fungi. The photograph shows Shaggy Pholiota *on an old beech, with an ancient pollard beyond.*

oak tortrix. The caterpillars can be so numerous in early summer that oak trees are stripped of all their leaves. The trees are unaffected by such defoliation and produce a new canopy of leaves in August. The only effect is a smaller annual growth ring. In similar fashion a host of fungi, beetles and flies is able to exploit the resources presented by an old tree. Indeed, nearly half of Britain's insect fauna is dependent upon standing dead wood. It was only in wood pasture that there was any continuity of mature timber and dead wood, but sadly only a few sites in Britain have escaped lean periods.

Lichens can be used as a barometer of the extent to which old forest species have been able to survive. A site well endowed with lichens known to be poor colonizers is very likely to support uncommon insects. The conditions which favoured the lichens also favoured dead-wood insects. Sadly, the reverse is not always true. Sites still important for dead-wood insects may have lost their lichens through air pollution and acid rain. Lichens are particularly sensitive to sulphur dioxide and as a result have survived best where there has been continuity of mature trees, relatively high humidity and moderately high light levels. Such areas are mainly in western Britain, where rainfall is highest and pollution is reduced by strong, clean, westerly winds.

There are some signs that local air pollution is ameliorating in southern England, for sensitive species have been observed to be growing well and others have reappeared in and around London many years after they had been eliminated by pollution.

Woods and butterflies

CRAB WOOD, HAMPSHIRE

Recently cut hazel coppice, with an old pollarded beech beyond, on a misty April morning.

Despite the growth of the newer traditions of forestry, which gradually replaced old-fashioned woodmanship, most woodland was coppiced well into the nineteenth century. Coppicing was already in decline by the time of the First World War but the exodus of working men from rural areas precipitated an irreversible nose-dive. The establishment of the Forestry Commission in

1919 provided a spur to even-aged plantation forestry and the Second World War was the final nail in the coffin of commercial coppicing. A much more recent revival of coppicing has only occurred as a result of desperate swimming against the tide by conservation bodies.

A well-managed mixed coppice woodland can support 300 to 400 species of higher plants and 2000 to 3000 species of invertebrates. The number of woody species present can be very impressive, and every one of them can have been coppiced.

A coppiced woodland displays a diverse ground flora, the combinations of species varying subtly in relation to soils and the length of time since the last cut. The cycle is well illustrated by the dog-violets. In the first year after coppicing, which is traditionally a winter activity, many violets are established from seed and are one of the first species to occupy bare ground. In their second year they grow rapidly and can be the most conspicuous species between the burgeoning coppice stools. In the third year they begin to suffer competition from common woodland plants like bluebell, honeysuckle and brambles. The decline continues in subsequent years. In the case of the dog-violet this cycle is of crucial importance to one of our more attractive butterflies, the pearl-bordered fritillary. The caterpillars of this species feed on violet leaves and the abundance of the dog-violet is thus an important factor controlling the production of the adult butterflies. Females lay their eggs on dead leaves or debris. When they hatch, the caterpillars set off in search of violets and will soon die if they fail to find any. Well before autumn they go into hibernation deep in leaf litter and in spring they awaken to resume the search for violets on which to feed.

It is not surprising that such a specialized and precarious life history is powerfully affected by changes in woodland management. Pearl-bordered fritillaries can cope very well with a short-rotation coppice cycle. The females show a strong preference for laying their eggs in two-year-old coppice, with a few using freshly cut areas. Any older coppice left to form a closed canopy is ignored. The abandonment of coppicing was therefore disastrous for the pearl-bordered fritillary. From being widespread throughout Great Britain and present in nearly every wood in southern England, it has declined steadily during the present century.

Other woodland insects

It is not surprising, when one thinks about the conditions which have prevailed since the last ice age, that it is only in woodland that insect communities come anywhere near their full potential for complexity. Woodland species had unlimited habitat and an abundance of tree species in a wide range of soils and climates. They evolved to fill all the niches presented by trees and many came to be exclusively associated with individual species.

There are many other adaptations and complexities within the insect groups. No wood is complete without its array of moths, beetles, bees, wasps, flies, plant bugs, aphids, lacewings and bush crickets with their multitude of predating and parasitic species. The non-insect invertebrates such as woodlice, centipedes, millipedes, spiders and harvestmen provide further tiers of interaction. There is apparently no limit to the ingenuity of nature, particularly with terrestrial invertebrates which have a rapid turnover of individuals, providing fertile material for evolutionary development.

A great many otherwise ecologically dull woods, including modern conifer plantations, only retain wildlife interest because the rides are kept open. Mowing and periodic cutting back of ride-sides may be labour-intensive but the wildlife benefits are considerable and it is a much easier option than maintaining a proper coppice rotation.

Rides provide sunny but sheltered conditions for insects that visit flowers, together with their predators and other associated species. Butterflies are among the more obvious beneficiaries but moths may be ten times as numerous.

The most valuable trees for insects are the oaks, birches and willows. Ecologists have proved that there is a very strong correlation between the numbers of insects associated with different trees and the relative abundance of those trees since the last ice age. Non-native species such as sycamore and sweet chestnut support small numbers of insects despite their abundance during the last few hundred years.

Birds and mammals

Red squirrel feeding.

Unlike plants or insects, birds can tell us very little about woodland history. They are highly mobile and respond immediately to the prevailing habitat or feeding conditions. They may vacate woodland but return just as quickly if conditions become favourable again. Many species use the different layers of woodland in their own way. Great tits, for example, nest in tree holes and collect food for their young in the woodland canopy. In winter they feed mainly on tree seeds but when these fall the birds follow them to the ground. Blue tits, on the other hand, are adept at searching the outermost parts of branches for insects, spiders and their eggs and only visit the ground as a last resort.

Woodpeckers listen intently for the sounds made by insect larvae as they excavate their tunnels within old wood. Once prey has been pinpointed, the woodpeckers have to start a chiselling operation requiring remarkable precision, strength and speed. The most expert is the great spotted woodpecker, a bird which is surprisingly common considering the high degree of specialization in its lifestyle. The resident birds are joined in spring by great numbers of migrants from Africa and southern Europe, flying north to exploit the sudden flush of insect food. These include several warblers, flycatchers, nightingale and redstart.

The pinewoods of the Scottish Highlands boast several important species, all of them with a rather specialized way of life. The crested tit hunts through the pine needles in search of small insects and spiders, while the intriguing crossbill, with its overlapping recurved mandibles, extracts seeds from pine cones. Needles, shoots, buds and young cones are all fair game for the huge capercaillie which was persecuted to extinction throughout the British Isles but was successfully reintroduced from continental stock in the 1830s.

Badger emerging from its woodland sett.

Most lowland woods have a well-established subterranean system of tunnels excavated by the mole, except in Ireland, where it never re-established itself after the last ice age, before the land bridge to Britain was closed by the rising sea. Moles have an ample supply of food in the form of earthworms and insect grubs, and a life relatively free from predators. They are not the only tunnellers, but woodmice, bank voles and badgers all have to come up to the woodland floor for the majority of their food. The small mammals are mainly

*T*his rare and beautiful plant stands amongst other spring flowers on the edge of a woodland nature reserve run by the Naturalists' Trust, on the Isle of Wight.

herbivorous, feeding on seeds, berries and shoots. Their only protection from predators is alertness, agility and speed, but these are qualities with which the stoat and weasel are also well equipped. Feeding mainly at night confers some advantage, though the tawny owl and the fox are very efficient nocturnal hunters. The dormouse is completely adapted to life in deciduous woodland. It avoids predators by seldom visiting the ground and remaining inconspicuous for the great majority of the time, deep in hibernation for about eight months and fast asleep for about eighteen hours per day during the rest of the year!

Deer are primarily woodland mammals, their main food being the leaves and shoots of trees and shrubs. The roe and the red deer are the only native species, but the red deer was driven from most of the lowlands and has learnt to cope with high-altitude moorland. Roe deer are common and increasing in much of lowland England, as are the introduced fallow and muntjac. Their numbers were previously kept under control by shooting and trapping but in most areas today they are unmolested, despite the problems they cause to foresters. Badgers, on the other hand, cause very few problems, despite their high numbers. Many sites have long-established setts with ten to twenty entrances and support two or three breeding sows. They enjoy a mixed diet of earthworms, insects, bulbs, roots and fruit.

The red squirrel must be the most popular of all woodland mammals, and is indeed very harmless compared with the introduced grey squirrel which has replaced it over most of the country. Red squirrels are managing to hold on in Scotland, parts of north Wales, northern England and Northern Ireland, particularly in coniferous forests where they have an advantage over the grey.

WISTMAN'S WOOD, DARTMOOR

*T*his is one of the strangest woods in the country, with gnarled dwarfed oaks, dripping with epiphytes, growing amongst moss-covered rocks. The oaks never grow larger than a few metres high, so the wood looks insignificant from a distance, yet the interior is another world.

DUNSTER DEER PARK, SOMERSET

*O*ld deer parks often contain wood pasture, with ancient trees, such as these venerable lichen-clad oaks, set in grazed pasture (right). The combination of ancient pollards or standard trees with unploughed grassland grazed by deer or livestock is more mediaeval than modern.

ASHAM WOOD, SOMERSET

*B*luebell woods are characteristically British and sights like this are rare elsewhere in Europe. Here, the bluebells are growing under ash and hazel coppice in a nature reserve on Carboniferous limestone in north Somerset. The neglected coppice is being gradually restored by the Naturalists' Trust.

FLY AGARICS

*T*he incredible colours of this fungus are a feature of birch woods in autumn when it comes up in masses after rain. The group shown here, demonstrating most of the stages of development, was photographed in light rain in a birch wood in Glen Almond, Tayside. The fungi, though beautiful, are poisonous and hallucinogenic and have also been used in the past as fly-killers (hence the name) among other things.

CLUMP OF WOOD VIOLET

*T*he photograph (above) was taken in Bradfield Woods, Suffolk, one of the most ancient and beautiful woods in Britain. This particular species of violet is one of a considerable number of plants growing here that indicate that the wood is very old.

SCALY MALE FERN

*T*he fronds of the fern, a good ancient woodland indicator in the south, are unfolding in an old oak wood in east Dorset. Further north, this species grows in a wider range of habitats.

PLANT LIFE ON AN OLD LOG

*T*he ancient woodlands in the deep coombes of Exmoor, support an exceptionally rich lichen, moss and liverwort flora, such as this beautiful mixture at Horner, West Somerset. The continuity of woodland cover, the presence of old trees, the high humidity and the relatively unpolluted air, combine to make this area ideal for these plants.

GROTON WOOD, CAMBRIDGESHIRE

A mass of wood anemones growing around the base of an ancient coppiced small-leaved lime (below). Small-leaved lime was once common in woods, but it is now rare. It is a good indicator of old woodland. Groton Wood is a Naturalists' Trust reserve.

BLACK WOOD OF RANNOCH, TAYSIDE

An old birch tree growing amongst pines (opposite). The Black Wood of Rannoch is a fascinating fragment of the ancient Caledonian pinewood on the shores of Loch Rannoch. Although described as 'pinewoods', these are really mixed woods, with birch, aspen, rowan and juniper amongst the larger pines.

HUMID BEECHWOOD, GLENCOE

There are masses of ferns (polypody), fungi (Russulas) and various mosses, liverworts and lichens growing on every surface. The beech trees are not thought to be native this far north, though the woods contain many typical northern plants and animals.

WESTER ROSS, NEAR LOCH TORRIDON

*I*nside an aspen wood on the west coast of Scotland (left). Aspen are pioneer trees, like birch, and they often form small woods in the far north, where more dominant trees are slow to oust them.

BIRCH WOOD FUNGI

*A*n attractive group of the *fungus* Galerina mutabilis *growing on an old birch trunk next to some cowberry berries in Craigellachie, Spey Valley, Cairngorms. In autumn, there are fungi everywhere in these old woods.*

CRAIGELLACHIE, SPEY VALLEY

*B*irch wood nature reserves in the Highlands are managed *as natural open woods, where trees lay as they fall, becoming homes for insects, fungi and other plants. This produces a more uneven-aged canopy, with plenty of sunny gaps for warmth-loving species.*

PINE FOREST REMNANT

*T*his remnant of ancient pine forest is by Loch Maree, Wester Ross in the Ben Eighe National Nature Reserve. Its open nature is clearly seen, with almost as much moorland as woodland.

WOOD ANTS' NEST

*T*his huge ants' nest is in pine woodland near Loch Garten in the Spey Valley, Scottish Highlands. Wood ants are an important component of many pine forest ecosystems (including plantations), and their distinctive heaped nests are a common sight.

FALLEN SCOTS PINE

*T*he Caledonian pine
forest fragments are
close to natural woodland,
where trees die and fall
naturally rather than when
they are harvested. This
makes the habitat much more
varied and interesting. This
particular pine, in the Black
wood of Rannoch, Tayside,
was used as a perch by a
male capercaillie.

RED SQUIRREL FOOD REMAINS

*T*hese discarded remains
(below), which give away
the presence of red squirrels,
were lying on a mossy carpet
in the pinewoods on
Brownsea Island, Poole
Harbour, Dorset. Brownsea
Island is one of the few places
in southern England where
red squirrels still occur. The
island is owned by the
National Trust and partly
managed as a Naturalists'
Trust reserve.

CRAB WOOD, HAMPSHIRE

*P*rimroses and bluebells growing in front of a pile of old coppice (left) that has recently been cut back to make the wood more suitable for flowers, birds and insects. The photograph was taken early on a misty April morning in Crab Wood, which is a Naturalists' Trust reserve.

HAYLEY WOOD, CAMBRIDGESHIRE

*T*he exceptional ground flora of Hayley Wood includes the rare true oxlip in masses, as well as bluebells, wood anemones and other common woodland flowers. The display of flowers in spring, before the tree canopy is fully open, is marvellous.

NORTHEND, AVON

A mass of wild garlic (ramsons) growing in an old hazel
coppice on the oolitic limestone near Bath. With this
amount of garlic, you usually smell it long before you see it! It
tends to form dense masses like this on base-rich damp clayey
soil, often close to rivers.

MARK ASH, NEW FOREST

These ancient beechwoods are known as the 'Ancient and Ornamental' (A & O) woods and they are all open to grazing by ponies and cattle under common rights, as well as herds of deer. The past history of their grazing can be 'read' from the present-day structure of the woods. They are amongst the most historic and interesting woods in Britain, despite their lack of flowers.

WOODLANDS

YOUNG COMMON TOAD

*I*t has recently emerged
from the nearby loch and is
taking cover under the fronds
of hard fern. Young toads
spread out widely after
emergence from a major
communal breeding site and
cover surprising distances.

LOWER KINGCOMBE, DORSET

*F*lowering blackthorn,
covered in lichens, catches
the early morning sun in a
thicket (below). At Lower
Kingcombe, a whole farm full
of unimproved meadows still
survives and part of the area
is now a nature reserve with
the Dorset Naturalists' Trust.
The whole area makes one
feel as though one has
stepped back fifty years.

SPEY VALLEY, SCOTTISH HIGHLANDS

*A*n intriguing view
(opposite) of some of the
birches in Craigellachie
nature reserve, with the
splash of red from an oddly
placed rowan seedling
contrasting with the lichen-
covered trunks of the downy
birches. Epiphytes such as
this, which are plants
growing on other plants, tend
to be commoner in the north
and west, where the humidity
and rainfall makes it easier
for them to survive.

PINNICK WOOD, NEW FOREST

*T*he ancient woods of the New Forest are mainly rather flowerless, due to centuries of grazing. However, a few areas, such as Pinnick, have a richer flora, though even here the flowers rarely occur in dense carpets. This picture (below) shows some wild daffodils.

SPRING ASH WOOD

*E*arly purple orchids (above) growing amongst the spring leaves of autumn crocus under hazel coppice in this beautiful ash wood on the limestone near Frome, Somerset. The abundance of both species in this wood is remarkable.

WHITE ADMIRAL

*T*his species (above) is confined to the woodlands of southern England. It is rather elusive and spends much of its time basking and drinking aphid honeydew high in the canopy.

GROUND IVY

*T*his flower is growing on an old elm stump in Knapwell Wood, Cambridgeshire – a Naturalists' Trust reserve, noted for its display of oxlips in spring.

GRASSLANDS

introduction by Susan Hampshire

I've always thought grasses were incredibly beautiful. They have a marvellous silhouette. Other plants have such dense foliage that you can't really appreciate the shape.

In towns, grassy places have a special value. Whenever I see a green patch in the city I feel calmed; I'm so happy to find these little pockets. It's inspiring and heartwarming to see the effort people have made to stop them being gobbled up by the advancing concrete.

All grass needs time and effort whether it's to save it from hypermarket proliferation or suffocation by scrub. The velvet bowling green, prized lawn and tennis court are prime examples of pampered grasses. But other wilder grasslands – hillsides, old pastures, roadsides and even village greens and parks are often taken for granted and not appreciated enough. And yet think what grass does for weary feet and how a picnic is enhanced on soft turf unsoiled by dogs.

Grass and grassland are the stuff of childhood summers. School picnics were held in Hyde Park and it always seemed sunny. Picnics were much less sophisticated affairs then but somehow seemed more enjoyable. We had huge doorstep sandwiches filled with some sort of squashed meat plus apples, cheese and tomatoes. Hyde Park seemed really quite rural in those days – no beer cans or bottles – and so much quieter. Traffic hummed gently in the background without the screeching intensity or the fumes and dust we get today.

Lying back you could watch the butterflies and bees and sunlight filtering through the leaves. And the grass was clean. Parks are no more than dogs' lavatories now. It was even safe to chew the stems then. Inside the older darker leaf was a succulent lime-green young one, furled like an umbrella. That was the best bit.

There were other picnics too – in the tawny hill grasslands of Wales and Scotland, surrounded by nodding harebells. These were quite different and always seemed to involve carrying lots of bags, and cows that nosed their way in. The family put stones in my bag so I wouldn't blow away. Once I fell off a stile and half way down a cliff which was pretty dramatic. We lit fires to cook on and sat down carefully to avoid the cowpats.

Different again were days at West Wittering on the Kent coast where we played cowboys and indians in the sand dunes. The coarse, wiry marram grass anchoring the volatile dunes in the face of the wind was a source of fascination and an important part of those summer days.

But it's not just traces of my past that run through the grass. Conservationist friends tell me about Port Meadow, near Oxford, a pasture full of beautiful wildflowers which has been grazed continuously since Domesday. One thousand years of stability. Well almost – apparently a hay crop was taken off it once in the Civil War. Port Meadow is a piece of living history as significant as the ancient buildings of Oxford itself. By spoiling it we would lose not only its beauty but a part of ourselves. Yet Port Meadow, like many other traditional pastures is under threat from abuse and misuse. Only if we learn to love and appreciate our grasslands will they remain to soothe our feet and refresh our senses.

Susan Hampshire

LITTONDALE, YORKSHIRE DALES

A glorious unimproved hay meadow photographed early one June morning.

Origins

There are no natural grasslands in Britain like the steppes of central Europe or the American prairies. Our climate is too favourable for the growth of trees, so that, if it is left alone, grassland will develop into scrub and eventually woodland. Despite this, a very significant proportion of Britain's wild plants and animals is associated with the short, managed habitats we call grassland. They have been created and maintained by man over many centuries. As farming practices stabilized, so too did the wildlife communities which found themselves able to coexist with man in this new open landscape.

Cutting and burning the forest had provided opportunities for many adaptable plants with good powers of dispersal. Many of these were annuals and biennials associated with disturbed ground. By grazing domestic animals, or taking a crop of hay to provide winter fodder, Neolithic man created new conditions in which grass species were usually dominant but where a wide range of broad-leaved plants could also thrive. The sward became closed, tightly-knit and composed very largely of perennial species.

TEESDALE HAY MEADOW

This extraordinary floral display was found in a hay meadow in Teesdale, above High Force. Melancholy thistle, wood cranesbill and pignut are the main species visible, amongst many others.

Silver-spotted skipper – a local butterfly of chalk downland.

Farming systems themselves evolved in response to soil and weather and, where a stable pattern of grass usage was maintained for a period of centuries, a distinctive community of plants and animals was created. This can be considered a man-made habitat but the range and distribution of native species within it is completely natural, so it is best described as 'semi-natural'. Most of the land surface of Britain was grazed by domestic animals during historic times and all but the most acid soils or exposed upland hillsides would have developed into some form of semi-natural grassland. Relatively few areas were maintained as grassland for long enough to become particularly species-rich, however, for woodland has been allowed to re-establish itself in some places; in other places, or at other times, the land has been used for growing crops. The action of ploughing, sowing and harvesting favours annual 'weeds', and is totally incompatible with the maintenance of semi-natural grasslands.

Herb-rich grassland was only able to develop on land which traditionally escaped the plough through being too wet, steep or exposed, the soils too poor for arable crops, or for peculiar reasons of tenure or law, for example common land. Only in areas like this would a long-established, stable community be able to survive, and only here could one expect to find plants with limited powers of dispersal and colonization. Devil's-bit scabious, saw-wort, dropwort, spiny restharrow, adder's-tongue and dyer's greenweed are examples of such indicators of old grassland. The number of such species in any site is limited by the age of the pasture, the general richness of grasslands on similar soils in the locality and also the extent to which the site has escaped damaging events such as periods of changing management.

Despite the vicissitudes caused by the historical ebbing and flowing of agricultural prosperity, lowland Britain was richly endowed with attractive herb-rich grasslands until the middle of the twentieth century. The varied geology and the range of regional farming methods ensured that different parts of the country had their own distinctive suites of semi-natural grasslands, such as chalk downland or wet flood meadows. They were a vital part of the landscape, contributing greatly to regional character, and were essential to the survival of many birds, butterflies and other animals.

Chalk and limestone grassland

When botanists analyse the floristic composition of grasslands, they find that even the most distinctive communites are part of an unbroken continuum. Chalk downland in Kent may look very different from limestone grassland in the Cotswolds or an old churchyard in the Midlands, but they all have a lot of species in common and it would be possible to find a string of sites in which the communities are intermediate.

One of Britain's most distinctive grassland types, and one for which we have a strong international responsibility, is chalk downland. It occurs in a great arc which sweeps from Dorset and Wiltshire through the Chilterns to Yorkshire, with a spur heading off to Surrey, Sussex and Kent. The rolling chalk hills were historically unenclosed and to this day they carry very few hedges. They were mostly used as sheep walks, with large flocks being slowly driven across them through the day and returned at night to pens on the arable where, in winter, they would have been fed rootcrops. Their dung was an important means of maintaining fertility.

Short, grazed grassland on thin chalk soils contains up to a dozen grass species but sheep's-fescue and meadow oat-grass are usually prominent. These and glaucous sedge give the turf a characteristic dull colour, contrasting starkly with the bright green of modern grass leys. Herb-rich chalk grassland typically contains as many as forty plant species in every square metre. Typical herbs include bird's-foot trefoil, horseshoe vetch, rock-rose, salad burnet, milkwort, fairy flax, squinancywort and thyme. All these and the many other plants are able to coexist because every species is under stress and unable to achieve its full potential. Each plant is held back by grazing, trampling, exposure, summer heat and drought, and by lack of nutrients. This last-named factor is of crucial importance because it is primarily the lack of available nitrogen and phosphorus which prevents more aggressive plants from dominating the community.

Limestone grassland occurs in a discontinuous belt from Somerset, through the Cotswolds to Yorkshire, Cumbria and Durham, with important outlying areas in both south and north Wales. Harder than chalk, the rock has eroded to produce steeper slopes, cliffs and rock outcrops which give the landscape a more rugged character. Bare rock is a feature of most sites, providing useful niches for specialized invertebrates such as spiders, and uncommon plants, including mosses and lichens.

Cumbria, Durham and the Yorkshire Dales contain some magnificent stretches of flowery grassland on carboniferous limestone, particularly at Whitbarrow Scar, Teesdale and Malham. This is the same rock as that which outcrops in the Derbyshire Dales, but it is a younger formation, the magnesium limestone, which runs in a long narrow band from Nottingham to Durham. The loss of semi-natural grassland to quarrying and agricultural improvements has been particularly severe on this rock type. New bare rock surfaces can greatly increase the scope for plants which require plenty of light but not too much competition, so that old quarries can become valuable places for lime-loving plants.

Skylark with nestlings.

Meadows

Almost any British plant can grow on a deep, lowland soil but most are prevented from doing so by competition. Management can reduce the vigour of the most aggressive plants and give a chance to the smaller ones. This process is exemplified by the process of hay cutting, in which material containing large quantities of plant nutrients is removed from the site every year. Further nutrients are removed by aftermath grazing (though a proportion is returned as dung) and the sward is taken down to a very low level before the stock are removed. When plants grow again in spring they all start from a similar low point, giving a chance to the less competitive.

Traditional hay meadows were once a common feature of wide, lowland river valleys, particularly those which were prone to flood or where the water table was normally too high for arable cultivation. The Thames meadows were perhaps the best known and there are still some magnificent examples on the outskirts of Oxford. It is believed that Pixey and Yarnton Meads have been mown for hay continuously for a thousand years. The best known of the rare and attractive plants associated with Thames hay meadows is the distinctive snake's head fritillary, whose large, nodding, mauve, chequer-board flowers appear *en masse* in late April.

*NORTH MEADOW
NATIONAL NATURE
RESERVE, WILTSHIRE*

*This is the finest
remaining example in
Britain of an unimproved
alluvial meadow with snake's
head fritillaries. There are
many thousands of fritillaries
here.*

The other part of the country renowned for its hay meadows is the
Yorkshire Dales. The richer lands in the valley bottoms were enclosed early
by dry stone walls and gradually a consistent form of management developed.
They were traditionally mown in late summer to provide hay as winter fodder
for dairy cows and the countless sheep which grazed the open fells.

Meadows which are too wet to permit a regular regime involving
agricultural machinery have escaped both ploughing and hay cutting. The
lack of cutting and a light stocking density usually allow rather more
structure to develop in the vegetation. The stock preferentially graze the driest
areas, which thus stay shorter and support a greater range of plants, while the
wetter and least grazed can grow quite tall and be dominated by a few erect
plants like rushes, pond-sedges, meadowsweet and meadow rue.

GRASSLANDS

AN UNIMPROVED WET MEADOW

The flora is dominated by marsh marigolds and ragged robin in a beautiful combination of colours. This example is in western Ireland where many such meadows still exist thanks to a lack of agricultural improvement.

Northern Ireland is particularly well endowed with wet grassland, for the climate is not well suited to cereal crops. Unfortunately, most of the land is in rather small agricultural holdings, and for farmers to achieve a reasonable standard of living it has been necessary to maintain high levels of production over the whole farm.

All the more extensive of the low-lying parts of the British Isles have been considered too valuable as resources to be used for only relatively unprofitable grazing by a few cows at the driest time of the year. Man had been tinkering with drainage in Britain since Saxon times but it was the Dutchman, Cornelius Vermuyden, in the seventeenth century, who cracked the enormous problem of draining the massive expanse of waterlogged peat in the Fens of Norfolk and Lincolnshire. This permitted a huge increase in grazing but the drainage was so successful and the ground so rich, that most of it was soon converted to arable. The exceptions to this are the huge ribbons of land known as the Ouse Washes and the Nene Washes, which were embanked as washland to receive flood water, whence it could be allowed to escape at a controlled rate into the tidal rivers.

Improvements in the techniques of drainage permitted the reclamation of other large wetlands and coastal saltings. A new and distinctive grassland landscape was created. The best known of these grazing marsh areas are in Broadland, the Somerset Levels, Romney Marsh, Pevensey Levels, north Kent,

the Essex coast and the Gwent Levels. Because the habitats are young in ecological terms and very different from what they replaced, the range of plants in the pasture is generally unimpressive.

The chalk valleys of southern England are fed by springs which maintain a slow but constant flow all the year round. These conditions make for good grazing and are very favourable to the survival of a rich array of grassland plants and animals, although very little of this land has been allowed to stay unmodified. Our resourceful eighteenth-century ancestors realized that they could manipulate the unusually well-behaved water to their advantage. By altering the contours of the meadows and creating a system of new channels they were able to allow water to flow slowly over the pasture. It could then be diverted to another part of the system before cattle were allowed in. The main benefits of this water-meadow management were the fertilizing effects of the water and protection from frost, thus promoting early spring growth for the cattle. Though obviously very much man-made, the habitat nevertheless supports a balanced mixture of species which interact with each other and the prevailing conditions in a purely natural way. Lady's smock, marsh ragwort and ragged robin are all features of water meadows.

A fairly constant assemblage of typical species characteristically occurs on the ridge-and-furrow grasslands of clay soils in the Midlands. These were created by ploughing the soil into parallel ridges which ensured, when they were subsequently grazed, that there was always some drier ground for stock to graze between the furrows. A high diversity of plant species can coexist in this sort of grassland, particularly where there has been continuity of heavy grazing over very many years. The grasses always occur as an intricate mixture, usually with plenty of red fescue, crested dog's-tail and sweet vernal-grass. The most frequent herbs are knapweed, cowslip, selfheal, yellow rattle, sorrel, lady's bedstraw and bulbous buttercup, with green-winged orchids often a very attractive feature.

Grassland mammals and birds

There are very few indigenous mammals which are primarily adapted to life in grassland. The strongest contender is the short-tailed vole, an endearing but retiring creature with a rounded nose and bright eyes. It requires rather tussocky grass and does not cope well with modern grass leys, but it is a prolific breeder and easily adapts in areas neglected for some time.

The most conspicuous mammals on the surface are likely to be rabbits. Certainly they can have a very beneficial effect in maintaining the diversity of semi-natural grassland, and many interesting sites lost their special features after rabbits were ravaged by myxomatosis in the 1950s. Hares are principally grassland creatures but they have adapted to life among cereal crops and can manage very well without permanent pasture.

A mammal which few people associate with grassland is the badger. Woodland badgers often leave the security of their setts to feed in grassland at night but others make a very good living in open ground such as chalk downland, well away from woodland.

Grasslands have a distinctive bird community. One of the most threatened is the corncrake, which has almost been eliminated but clings to survival in Northern Ireland and western Scotland, particularly in Hebridean meadows. It relies on low-intensity traditional farming, just the sort of land management

A young rabbit.

which *should* be subsidized by the European Community. The quail is more of a lowland species and consequently did not have the option of retreating north and westwards in the face of agricultural improvement. It is an uncommon inhabitant of rough grassland and cereal fields. Other birds are rather more conspicuous, like the lapwing, curlew, snipe and redshank, and of course the grey partridge is primarily a grassland bird. The stone curlew is a rare breeding bird of southern and eastern England. A few pairs nest in unimproved chalk grassland with very thin soil and patches of bare ground, but most of them choose to nest in late-sown arable crops where the ground is bare during March and April. Grassland song birds, notably the skylark and meadow pipit, may nest in all but the most intensively managed grass.

Grassland insects

An enormous array of invertebrates can be found in grassland. In terms of numbers alone it is ants which are likely to dominate but the bulk of the species are contributed by moths, beetles, flies, plant bugs and spiders. However, naturalists have in the past devoted a great deal of skill and dedication to the study of grassland butterflies. This has been extended by recent much-needed scientific research, for the decline of many species has been alarming, particularly those associated with chalk grassland. The reason for the intense interest in butterflies is obvious, for their grace and beauty have been a source of inspiration for centuries. The life histories of these creatures are no less fascinating than their beauty. For example, the adonis blue has an intimate relationship with ants and cannot complete its life without them. The larvae and pupae produce a sugary secretion which is 'milked' by ants. In return, the larvae are afforded protection by the ants, which actually cover them at night to hide them from predators. The larvae feed in daylight hours on the leaves of horseshoe vetch, still attended by ants.

The fate of semi-natural grassland

It is a sad fact that the proportion of semi-natural grassland which has been destroyed in recent decades is far greater than that of any other habitat. The drive to produce more food during the Second World War meant that a great many areas of old downland and meadow, including many commons, were ploughed up, possibly for the first time in centuries. The post-war government embarked on a massive programme to increase agricultural efficiency by means of grants, loans and technical advice based on scientific research. The use of inorganic fertilizers and pesticides was enormously increased and land drainage became a major industry. The policy was hugely successful in increasing productivity and profitability and very little farmland has escaped the drive for agricultural intensification. The few areas of pasture which escaped ploughing, drainage or reseeding seldom also escaped fertilizing. Between the 1940s and the 1980s, 95% of Britain's semi-natural grassland was destroyed. Most of the land which has survived is in small parcels which happened to escape through some accident of history, perhaps a long period of benevolent or inefficient management in the hands of a die-hard owner/occupier, or because the land was too steep, wet or inaccessible to warrant the necessary effort.

Common land status has been particularly helpful in protecting grassland from agricultural improvement but by no means all of it has continued to receive the low-intensity grazing which is necessary for the maintenance of its scientific interest.

A very impressive array of important sites is being maintained in nature reserves and other areas which are not subject to agricultural improvement. Country parks, public open spaces, military training areas, water catchment areas and churchyards all provide valuable havens for grassland wildlife. All have to be maintained by some form of management otherwise they will change into coarse, species-poor grassland and eventually scrub. Grazing is the ideal but this is not always possible. Many areas are mown, most of them rather too frequently. Unfortunately, in very few places are the cuttings removed, an inconvenient but essential prerequisite for a significant increase in botanical diversity. Periodic disturbance is one way of maintaining grassland, and this is what happens on some military training areas. The occasional passage of tanks, or even regular but dispersed bombardment with explosive shells is actually quite an effective way of maintaining species-rich grassland!

BURLEY, NEW FOREST

Amongst the many habitats to be found in the New Forest are the 'lawns' – grassy clearings in the ancient woodland, which have been grazed by deer and ponies for centuries.

GRASSLANDS

LOCH DIABAIGAS, ROSS AND CROMARTY

A beautiful herb-rich hay meadow running down to Loch Diabaigas, just north of Loch Torridon. Even in north-west Scotland, there are now few flowery hay meadows left, as most have been agriculturally improved by spraying or fertilizing. Most of this area is simply unenclosed rough pasture, as can be seen from the far shores of the loch, with this hay meadow as one of the few splashes of bright colour in the landscape.

MONEWDEN MEADOWS, SUFFOLK

*T*hese meadows are some of the most species-rich and oldest that are known. In spring, the sward is a mass of orchids, cowslips and other plants; by midsummer, the grasses take over (above) in a beautiful mass of more subtle colours, with a number of species represented. After the hay is cut, there is a late summer display of autumn crocus (opposite), one of our most attractive native flowers. Strangely, the fruits do not ripen fully until the spring when they reappear with the leaves, which themselves die back long before flowering.

GREEN-VEINED WHITE BUTTERFLY

*T*he butterfly is feeding on a cats ear flower in a hay meadow in Ribblesdale, North Yorkshire. Relatively few butterflies breed in hay meadows, because the cutting interrupts their life cycle. However, many visit the flowers for nectar and they often breed around the edges of the meadows.

HERB-RICH SWARD, SELWORTHY

*C*emeteries and graveyards often contain fragments of old meadowland, such as this beautiful sward at Selworthy, Somerset (left). It is dominated by red clover, cats ear and other flowers.

MULL, WEST SCOTLAND

*A*n old field gateway (opposite), with whitebeam, roses, male fern and brambles growing around and through it. The luxuriant vegetation is a feature of sheltered parts of west Scotland, and is due to the high rainfall and mild climate.

DANDELIONS, NORTH WILTSHIRE

*D*andelion-dominated *fields rarely contain much else of interest except dandelions, but they are a beautiful sight nonetheless, and a disappearing one (above and right). They most commonly appear in a sward with high nutrients, a few years after ploughing.*

LAX-FLOWERED ORCHIDS, GUERNSEY

Within the British Isles, this orchid only occurs on the Channel Islands in damp unimproved meadows. Here (opposite), they are growing on Guernsey, on a Société Guernsiaise reserve. Many such meadows have disappeared, with most of the remaining plants only existing in nature reserves. Behind the flowers, the unusual reed 'hedge' is visible.

SUTTON HOLMS MEADOW, DORSET

Bistort growing in one of the few old meadows left in Dorset, now managed as a Naturalists' Trust reserve for its marvellous mixture of flowers. The photograph was taken very early one June morning, before the dew had gone and before any breeze had got up.

LIMESTONE GRASSLAND, SOUTH GLOUCESTERSHIRE

*T*his is an early spring display of cowslips and daisies. The
grasslands on the oolitic limestone of the Cotswolds are
very similar to chalk downs in the character of their flora and
in their management by sheep grazing.

COMMON BLUE BUTTERFLY

*I*n cooler weather, chalk downland butterflies, such as this common blue (above), may bask on bare chalk to receive the most warmth. This male is on the chalk downs at Broughton Down, Hampshire, a Naturalists' Trust reserve.

WHITE ROCK-ROSE

*T*he hard Carboniferous limestone, where it outcrops, gives rise to a fascinating mixture of turf and rock gardens, often with rare plants such as this white rock-rose at Brean Down, Somerset, owned by the National Trust. This is one of the few British sites where this species can be found.

GRASSLANDS

ROADSIDE SPLENDOUR IN HAMPSHIRE

A striking mixture of annual weeds growing on a roadside and spreading across into the adjacent field. The intense red of the common poppies is further intensified by the misty morning light, contrasting with the orange-yellow of corn marigolds. Scattered amongst these two species, there are smaller quantities of ox-eye daisy, white campion, hairy tare and yorkshire fog. Modern seed-cleaning and treatment methods have made sights such as these rare, and they are now only to be seen either where mistakes are made or on non-agricultural land, especially where new roads cut through a bank.

GRASSLANDS

WILD THYME AND DINGY SKIPPER

The thyme is surrounded by wild strawberries and is being visited by a dingy skipper butterfly, in a disused limestone quarry. Sheltered old quarries on chalk and limestone are often surprisingly rich in species. This photograph was taken at the Naturalists' Trust reserve, Millers Dale, Derbyshire.

IONA OFF SCOTLAND'S WEST COAST

A mixed flock of rooks and hooded crows feeding avidly on stooks of oat straw on a breezy autumn day.

DUNSTER, WEST SOMERSET

The anthills produced by the yellow meadow ant are a feature of old, unploughed grassland, such as these in the ancient deer park at Dunster. Their size is a good indication of the age of the grassland, since they steadily increase in size with time; ploughing, or various other agricultural activities, destroys them.

DRYSTONE WALL, HANDA ISLAND

A single frond of bracken sprouting from an old wall (above). The drystone walls in west Scotland give an added dimension to the habitat for both plants and animals.

RIBBLESDALE, YORKSHIRE

More acid meadows in the dales have a different flora. This meadow is dominated by the white flowers of pignut, together with sheep's sorrel, mat grass and a few other species. They are generally neither as rich in species nor as colourful as those on more lime-rich soil.

LAPWING'S NEST, NORTH OXFORDSHIRE

*T*his herb-rich pasture (below) was photographed late on a summer evening. Lapwing frequently nest in old pastures grazed by stock, where the open sward suits their needs.

UPPER TEESDALE HAY MEADOW

*D*ales hay meadows are important biologically, but also beautiful to look at, with their combination of natural colour and man-made buildings and walls. This particular example (above) is within the Upper Teesdale National Nature Reserve.

HARDINGTON MEADOW, SOMERSET

A superb example of *unimproved enclosed pasture on the base-rich hills of south Somerset. In this area, most pasture is now heavily improved for the intensive dairy industry, but here and there meadows and pastures have escaped the drive towards greater productivity. The photograph shows a glorious combination of green-winged orchids and cowslips (both once-common, but now increasingly uncommon), together with a few bulbous buttercups, all at their peak of flowering in mid-May.*

103

WETLANDS
introduction by Bill Oddie

Nearly all my favourite birdy memories involve watery places. When I was a small schoolboy, every weekend, I used to leap onto my flashy drop-handlebar bike with my binoculars safely round my neck and my telescope dangling dangerously close to the spokes and tazz off to Bartley Reservoir on the outskirts of Birmingham.

Here I first experienced the thrill of being chased off private land by the water bailiff and his slavering alsatian after I'd dared to slip through the railings to get a closer view of a curlew that was taking an equal risk trying to plunge its beak into a solid concrete shoreline. Near by, I also first learnt how any little damp patch can attract migrant songbirds as I struggled to separate willow warblers from chiffchaffs and sedge from reed warblers as they flitted through the willows and reeds at a splendid little overgrown pond at Westminster Farm.

When my dad acquired his first car, my wetland experiences diversified accordingly. I persuaded him to take our summer holiday in Norfolk. We watched herons guarding fenland ditches, we flushed a bittern from almost beneath our feet at Hickling Broad and I saw all manner of new waders at often tantalizing distances on the then largely private and inaccessible scrapes and flashes across Cley Marshes.

Then I passed my driving test. Dad decided he preferred the risk of lending me his car to the boredom of carting me around and waiting whilst I disappeared for hours on end looking for birds. Each Sunday morning I'd rev away at dawn, leaving a note telling him I was 'just nipping over to Bartley'. In truth, I used to cover a circuit of most of the water in the west Midlands!

Since then I've travelled the world, and if I had to name my most absorbing birding experience anywhere ever, I think I'd have to nominate my first visit to Bharatpur in India. Yes, another wetland, and one which perfectly illustrates the magic of such places. For a start, the whole atmosphere is incredibly beautiful. Then there's the birds: all manner of wildfowl and waders tracing patterns in the sky as they fly, sometimes so profuse in their flocks that you can hardly separate individuals, and filling the air with weird and wonderful sounds. But not just water birds. Birds of prey: marsh harriers or peregrine falcons

patrolling and stooping, scattering a thousand panicking wings. And the little birds: warblers and flycatchers cascading after insects in the damp bushes. And how about the insects themselves? Dazzling dragonflies, beautiful butterflies . . . and the flowers they feed on: orchids and irises, bulrushes and sedges . . . and beneath them . . . the aquatic life. The truth is that there is nowhere – just nowhere – where the sheer variety of natural life is better encapsulated than in wetland habitats. Be it in India, Norfolk . . . or a short bike ride outside Birmingham!

These days it is sadly almost obligatory, when invited to contribute to a book like this, to bemoan the loss of our most valuable habitats. Certainly wetlands *are* under the most dreadful threats. Not only has my own little local patch at Westminster Farm been filled in but so too have many much larger patches. Hardly a week passes but that we read of plans to build dams and barrages euphemistically 'reclaiming' or 'improving' marshes and estuaries. 'Destroying' would be the more honest and distressing word. However, all is not gloom. I recently revisited Bartley and found a 'Nature Reserve' sign adorning the local woodland and observation benches overlooking the reservoir. Even the water bailiff's dog panted amiably. The Norfolk coast is now almost entirely reserved for fauna and flora and delightfully accessible to the nature-loving public. Last year I went back to Northumberland to open more wetland sites that had been created by filling up some of the scars caused by open-cast mining; and in Suffolk I visited disused gravel pits that had been similarly transformed. The fact is that whilst we must indeed preserve every inch of natural wetland habitat we have left, we do also have the opportunity of literally creating areas that can eventually be equally productive to wildlife. The Wildfowl Trust, the RSPB, various county trusts and so on, with the cooperation of some of the more enlightened industrial companies, are achieving just that. So, if I may coin a phrase, when it comes to wetlands, 'there's not only natural Britain . . . there's un-natural Britain as well'. I hope you enjoy both as much as I do.

Bill Oddie

HIGHLAND STREAM IN TAYSIDE

Rapids and falls in a stream in the Black Wood of Rannoch, on the shores of Loch Rannoch.

Life in fresh water

Wetlands include lakes, ponds, marshes, fens, bogs, rivers and streams. Few parts of Britain are lacking in such habitats and no one should have to travel far to appreciate the variety of plants and animals adapted to life in fresh water. The first faltering steps of evolution took place in a watery environment, and it was only yesterday in geological time that vertebrates first dragged themselves onto dry ground. It is not surprising, therefore, that aquatic plants and animals display such a formidable array of forms and adaptations. Some animals, such as fish, are wholly aquatic; some, such as otters, water shrews, diving ducks, grebes and water beetles, are adapted equally well to water and air; there are those, such as frogs, dragonflies, mayflies and mosquitoes, which have aquatic larvae but airborne adults; and others are not strictly aquatic at all but are nevertheless able to exploit the rich food potential of water. These include the osprey, kingfisher, many species of duck, grass snake and water spider.

A new pond provides convincing evidence that nature abhors a vacuum. Airborne spores soon initiate a population of free-floating, single-celled green algae, capable of doubling their numbers every thirty minutes. Examination of a single drop of water will reveal that the algae are soon supporting a population of water fleas or other microscopic animals and these in turn will provide sustenance for various larger invertebrates. More complex algae then appear, followed by rooted higher plants. Before long, dragonflies, frogs, toads, newts and birds discover the pond, and even fish may appear, perhaps flown in with the mud on ducks' feet.

In reality a pond offers relatively restricted opportunities for plants and animals but it provides a hint of the potential richness and productivity of freshwater habitats. Large numbers of species may coexist where the density

SALMON JUMPING, TAYSIDE

Two salmon simultaneously making a desperate jump up a waterfall in spate. Autumn is the peak period for jumping, as the fish make their way up-river to spawn.

DIPPER IN MID-STREAM

These energetic birds are typical of fast-flowing rocky streams where they feed on aquatic invertebrates. They have developed the ability to walk along the stream bed under the water, searching for prey.

of floating algae, the phytoplankton, is kept low so that the water remains clear, letting light penetrate to the bottom. This enables rooted aquatic plants to flourish and they, in turn, multiply the opportunities for other organisms. The diversity of plants and animals is much greater if the water body never dries out, if there is an adequate supply of oxygen and dissolved plant nutrients, if it is large enough to avoid sudden changes in temperature and deep enough never to freeze solid. A steady inflow and gentle water movement may increase the scope for some species, but sudden rushes of storm water into a small body of water are likely to prove damaging. A healthy lowland lake will support a complex ecosystem with a range of higher plants and algae, high densities of herbivorous animals, such as water fleas and water snails, many creatures which live in or on the bottom scavenging off the organic particles which drift gently down from the surface layers, active predators such as the larvae of dragonflies and the larger water bugs, fish which range in size and type from the humble minnow to enormous pike, and birds which may feed on water weeds, invertebrates or fish.

Natural lakes

Most of Britain's standing and flowing waters have been modified by man but there are still a great many sites which can legitimately be regarded as natural. The majority of natural lakes are of glacial origin, occupying hollows left in the undulating landscape created by retreating ice-sheets. It is not difficult to imagine the scouring action of a glacier, gouging out a high mountainside and depositing a great mound of debris as it melted.

THE RIVER DEE NEAR BALMORAL

The River Dee, flowing east from the Cairngorms, is a fine example of a large upland river, rich in life. In the distance, the mountains of Lochnagar, made famous by Prince Charles, can be seen.

The great sheets of water in the Lake District, some of which are very deep, originated in this way. The lakes occupy the huge U-shaped valleys created by ice-age glaciers and plugged at the outfall end by the glaciers' burden of rock and debris known as glacial till. The water is fairly acid and lacking in plant nutrients, and the shorelines are often subject to severe wave action. Most of the lakes therefore have little in the way of submerged aquatic plants or fringing marshy vegetation.

The undulating countryside of Cheshire and Shropshire contains a fascinating series of lakes and bogs known as meres and mosses. Their origin may not be so easy to visualize, but they too were created by the physical extremes of the ice ages. Massive ice-sheets ground their way remorselessly downhill until periods of thaw resulted in sudden violent erosion. The result, in the present interglacial period, is an irregular landscape of mounds and hollows. The deepest of these hollows were caused by deposition of till around massive ice-blocks which melted at a later date. Lakes formed in this way, such as Crose Mere and Oak Mere, are known as kettle-holes.

The majority of the many lakes in Northern Ireland appeared at the end of the last glaciation, and the Upper Lough Erne area, which is an extraordinary complex of mostly rather small, irregularly shaped lakes, is best explained by the kettle-hole concept.

A minority of the meres of Cheshire and Shropshire have a different origin. They are situated over the Cheshire salt rock beds, a natural deposit laid down earlier in geological time by the evaporation of water from an ancient sea. Over a very long time-scale the salt has been dissolved and carried away by water, allowing the overlying deposits to slump. The resulting depressions have filled with water to produce yet more lakes.

The Cheshire meres and most upland lakes are situated on impermeable layers of rock and are independent of any water beneath the ground. Lakes in other parts of Britain, however, often lie on permeable materials such as limestone, chalk or sand and their depth is a direct reflection of the height of the water table in the underlying deposits. If the water table drops below the level of the lake bed, the lake dries up. When the subterranean water levels rise, possibly as a result of rainfall some distance away, the lake reappears. The Breckland meres, on the Norfolk/Suffolk border, are lakes of this sort and they are all the more intriguing for the unpredictability of their fluctuations.

The finest examples of naturally fluctuating lakes are without question the turloughs of County Clare in Ireland. Here the grassy swards revealed by the widely fluctuating water levels have been subject to light grazing for countless generations. The turloughs support an extraordinary community of plants including an abundance of the very rare fen violet.

The sea around Britain has had many dramatic changes of level over the last few hundred thousand years. During the last ice age, for example, so much water was locked up in the huge ice-sheets of the northern hemisphere that the sea was as much as 100 metres below its present level. Britain was joined to the continent by a wide land bridge which was not finally breached until about 9000 years ago. The rising sea flooded vast areas of land, producing new expanses of estuarine mud and saltmarsh over what was formerly dry land. When the sea was later excluded from some of these areas, perhaps by the formation of a bar of sand or shingle, combined with falling sea levels, new fresh-water lakes or marshes developed. It is events of this sort which account for the very extensive wetlands known as the Somerset Levels.

The early history of the area known as Broadland, in eastern Norfolk and Suffolk, is not dissimilar to that of the Somerset Levels. Fen peat had accumulated as a result of the vigorous growth of reedswamp during periods of high water levels. When the sea dropped to a level known to be about four metres below the present, the marshes dried sufficiently to enable a peat-cutting industry to develop and thrive from the tenth to the thirteenth century. The demand for peat is known to have been very great at this time. A subsequent rise in sea-level made the peat cuttings very difficult to work and they were eventually abandoned in 1287 after a great flood. The lakes, or Broads as they are known, are therefore actually man-made, straight-sided, flooded pits. Over time they acquired such a natural aspect that their true origin was not deduced until the 1950s. Unfortunately, in recent decades, a great deal of the natural interest of the Broads has declined. It is thought that this is due to eutrophication resulting from run-off from arable land, increasing phosphate levels in the rivers from sewage works and the effect of motorboats on the water turbity and river banks.

Rivers and streams

Rivers are an important element of many landscapes, from steep rugged mountainsides, through rolling hill country to wide lowland floodplains. They have helped to form the landscape and they still exert a major influence on the wildlife of the land that they drain. Within their waters, however, a relentless flow normally prevents the development of planktonic life. On the other hand, oxygen levels are high in running waters and conditions for plants and invertebrate animals can be very favourable, provided they have a means of avoiding being swept away by the current. The violent torrents of mountain streams support only a few specialized invertebrates and mosses but diversity increases rapidly with more gentle gradients, slower flows, higher temperatures and greater supplies of nutrients. Upland, as opposed to mountain, rivers with rock-strewn rapids alternating with calm pools, produce very interesting habitats, with more diverse invertebrate communities, a few fish and such attractive birds as dipper, common sandpiper and grey wagtail.

BOG MOSS

*T*his photograph from Loch Maree shows the glorious mixture of colours to be found on an active bog surface in unpolluted west Scotland, where several species of Sphagnum moss grow together.

A cluster of mating common toads.

Yet more species are present further down the streams and in lazy, meandering, lowland rivers. Broad fringes of the emergent vegetation which the slower-moving water allows can support a very high diversity of plants and insects. This is the spawning ground for many coarse fish and provides nest sites and feeding habitats for many birds.

Apart from differences produced by altitude and water chemistry, rivers can be divided into two broad types. There are those which are situated on impermeable rock or clay and which therefore rise rapidly after rainfall because surface run-off soon reaches the river. By contrast, surface run-off is almost non-existent for rivers on permeable deposits, because all rainwater seeps into the ground. The rivers here are fed by springs, which are low points where the groundwater reappears at the surface. If the supply of groundwater is large enough, the springs will be unaffected by short-term rainfall and will flow all the year. The classic spring-fed rivers are the chalk streams of southern England, with crystal-clear water, gravel bottoms and an abundance of white-flowered water crowfoot. These rivers are fed by a steady supply of water which is extraordinarily constant in chemical composition and temperature, relatively cold in summer and warm in winter.

'Flashy' clay rivers, on the other hand, rise rapidly after storms and their beds are scoured out by the violence of the water. In summer the flow may drop dramatically, the temperature rises and the dissolved nutrients (or pollutants) may become very concentrated. Some clay rivers, such as the Avon, which empties into the Severn estuary near Bristol, are so variable that their flow in spate can be over a thousand times that during dry weather. The physical and chemical limitations on plants and animals can therefore be very severe. However, they have had a long time to adapt to life in flashy rivers and a great many species have found effective means of coping with the difficulties. In fact, the banks of such rivers may be very colourful, with many hoverflies and damselflies playing around the fringing flowers.

Large areas of reedswamps are to be found where a river meets the sea. If its path is blocked by a natural bar or a tidal sluice, such as at Minsmere in Suffolk or Radipole Lake in Dorset, the impounded fresh water may be invaded by reed up to two metres tall. All the large reed beds in southern England hold colonies of reed warblers, usually with their attendant cuckoos.

Man-made wetlands

Ever since prehistoric times man has been tinkering with natural wetlands or creating new ones. An interesting example of the latter is the canal. In the seventeenth century a spate of canal-building began, to provide cheap transport for bulky materials. One of the earliest canals to be built was the Basingstoke Canal, but its use for commercial traffic was very short-lived; for nearly 300 years it was very little used other than by the many plants and animals which were able to colonize its water and marshy fringes. Although the majority of canals still survive, their traffic is now purely recreational and the aquatic community, where it has not been eliminated by excessive numbers of powered boats, has more in common with lakes than with rivers.

From medieval times, lakes were created to provide fish, a head of water to drive mills, or to enhance the landscape of ornamental parks and gardens. Some of these have acquired a relatively stable, semi-natural community of plants and animals. Another wetland habitat to have appeared in the last two centuries has been the shallow lakes and marshes which result from subterranean collapses of worked-out mines. Some of these, such as Stodmarsh in Kent, have been colonized by reedswamp and a rich variety of plant and animal life. It is equally likely that some of the many gravel-pit lakes, which are being continuously created to supply the construction industry, will eventually become as interesting as much older wetlands.

Peatlands

Most plant material which grows in wetland habitats starts to decompose when it dies down and has disappeared within a few years. This does not occur, however, if bacterial activity is frustrated by lack of oxygen, and this can happen if the material is kept constantly wet but without any flow of water. In these conditions the material may break into smaller particles while still retaining much of its original structure and composition. Each year further material is added, compacting that below into dark, waterlogged peat. A wide range of important habitats results from this process. Collectively, these habitats are known as mires, but they can be split into two broad groups, depending on their water chemistry. Sites which are fed by mineral-rich groundwater are known as fens whereas sites which are away from the influence of such groundwater and are fed either by acid, base-poor water or alternatively just by rainwater are known as bogs. These are most likely to develop in areas of high rainfall, high humidity and cool summer temperatures. The bogs of central Ireland represented the finest development of this habitat in Europe but most of them have been destroyed by commercial peat cuttings. Almost one-third of Northern Ireland had peat soils but today most of the extensive moorland and bog has been radically altered by drainage, turf cutting and grazing. The origin of most of this bog goes back to the Atlantic period, 6000–3000 BC, when the climate became warmer and wetter, and sea and lake levels rose. *Sphagnum* mosses overwhelmed the former woodland of birch and pine.

In Wales and Scotland much peatland has been destroyed through drainage and afforestation but fortunately many fine peatlands still survive throughout the British Isles. They are very extensive in the uplands but they can also occur at low altitude and in a climate as equable as that of East Anglia, Hampshire or Dorset. The New Forest contains the finest collection of lowland valley bogs but there are other magnificent examples at Roydon Common in Norfolk, Thursley Common in Surrey and the Hartland/Arne area in Dorset.

Another kind of mire, known as a raised bog, occurs at low altitude in areas of high rainfall such as Northern Ireland, west Wales and a few places in Scotland. The bog adjacent to Malham Tarn in North Yorkshire has been studied by generations of students at the Field Studies Centre.

The plants and animals of bogs are generally very different from those of fens, though a few species may occur in both. Bogs normally look distinctive because *Sphagnum* often comprises a large proportion of the vegetation. A rich, undamaged bog can contain up to about fifteen species of *Sphagnum*, various other mosses and liverworts, cotton-grass, a few sedges and related species, ericaceous plants like heather, cross-leaved heath and cranberry, and various broad-leaved plants, such as sweet gale, creeping willow, bog asphodel and the insectivorous sundews and butterworts. The ability to entrap and digest insects has evolved in various plants of bogs and fens in

Grey heron fishing in a reed-filled ditch.

The great crested grebe has been quick to colonize the numerous flooded gravel pits that have appeared in lowland Britain in recent years.

The bogs of western and central Ireland are famous, and those of Connemara in the wet far west are particularly extensive. They are cut for peat everywhere, which is used as a substitute for coal.

response to the lack of available nitrogen. These plants are able to obtain all the nutrients they require from the bodies of the unfortunate insects. Where surface water movement occurs, the supply of nutrients is increased a little, so permitting the growth of other species like bog St John's wort, bog pondweed and marsh violet.

There are a few insect species which are specialist bog inhabitants, the most notable being the bog bush cricket and the large marsh grasshopper, which are both spectacular insects, being large, distinctive and brightly coloured. The grasshopper has the sensible but very annoying habit of letting go to drop out of sight at the approach of danger. Several dragonflies may be seen hunting over bogs, notably the keeled skimmer, the black darter and the small red damselfly. The majority of invertebrate animals on a bog surface are in fact spiders.

Like bogs, fens receive a very constant supply of water but in this case it is rich in base elements, notably calcium and magnesium. Most fens are fed by groundwater, which is able to move laterally through permeable material but is prevented from moving downwards by an impermeable layer such as clay.

Botanically rich fens have a very limited distribution, primarily in Norfolk, Anglesey and Oxfordshire. The dominant plants are usually blunt-flowered rush or one of the larger sedges of the genus *Carex*. The common reed is often present but only dominates where nutrient levels are higher. Typical species of rich fen, a diverse and very attractive community of low plants, are marsh valerian, fen bedstraw, red rattle, bog pimpernel, bogbean, marsh pennywort, common butterwort, marsh helleborine, fragrant orchid, southern and early marsh orchids and various mosses.

113

LOCH MALLACHIE, SPEY VALLEY

*T*he attractive Loch Mallachie lies deep in the Abernethy forest, in the Spey Valley in the highlands of Scotland. Much of the surrounding forest is ancient Caledonian pine woodland and the whole area is beautiful and unspoilt. Loch Garten, famous for its breeding ospreys, lies nearby, and both lakes are within a Royal Society for the Protection of Birds reserve. Loch Mallachie is smaller and more sheltered than Loch Garten, with a more varied insect life, though the whole area is especially rich in all forms of wildlife. The photograph was taken at about 10.30 p.m. on a July evening, utilizing the last of the light from the amazingly long Scottish summer days.

BOTTLE SEDGE AND WATER HORSETAIL

*N*either sedges nor horsetails (left) are normally viewed as being especially attractive, but this mixture of the two, photographed soon after dawn with a heavy covering of dew is stunning. This is a typical mixture of plants to be found in wet, nutrient-poor fens.

SMALL RED DAMSELFLY

*T*his is one of only two species of red damselfly that occurs in Britain. It is found rather sparingly in bogs in heathland areas in the south and west. Its red legs help to separate it from the large red, which has black legs. This one was photographed in a Surrey bog.

LOCH AN EILEANN, SCOTLAND

*T*he beautiful Loch an Eileann is set like a blue jewel in the
dark green of the Rothiemurchus pine forest. It is
completely unspoilt and, as the photograph shows, the margins
are a lovely mixture of marsh, forest, and open scrub, with
juniper in the foreground. It lies within the Cairngorm
National Nature Reserve.

BY THE RIVER WYE, PEAK DISTRICT

*A*n attractive mixture *(opposite) of riverside flowers, mainly water avens and meadowsweet, in Millersdale, Peak District National Park. The Photograph was taken late on a June evening.*

MONKEY MUSK BY THE RIVER RIBBLE

*A*whole mass of monkey *flower (left) lines the banks and channels of a nearly dry River Ribble, in the Yorkshire Dales. An introduced species, the musk has found its own niche and exploited it fully.*

LANGDON BECK, UPPER TEESDALE

*A*n unspoilt small upland *river, running down into the Tees, within the Upper Teesdale National Nature Reserve. The banks are lined with flowery meadows and pastures.*

LOCH CLAIR, THE SCOTTISH HIGHLANDS

A beautiful example of a large unspoilt west-highland loch, with masses of fringing and emergent plants, such as sedges, horsetails and water Lobelia. There are remnants of Caledonian pine wood on the far slopes and the hills behind are the Forest of Coulin.

WATER HORSETAILS IN A HIGHLAND LOCH

An evening view of the stems of masses of water horsetails emerging from a loch in Sutherland, north-west Scotland. The horsetails are non-flowering plants, related to ferns, but an important part of many wetland communities.

A LOCH ON RANNOCH MOOR

The photograph shows the rocky margin of a loch on Rannoch moor, not far from Glencoe, Scotland. Around the moss and lichen-covered boulders there are masses of lesser spearwort flowers, lit up by the evening sun. Less conspicuously, there are also sedges, rushes and horsetails in the loch-edge community.

SUNDEWS IN A CHESHIRE BOG

*S*undews are insectivorous *plants that catch insects on their sticky red hairs, then digest them with secreted enzymes. Most British insect-eating plants live in acid bogs, where their special mode of life gives them an added advantage, in terms of extra nutrients, over their competitors, in a difficult environment. This group of common sundews was growing on the surface of a floating raft of bog moss on a reserve in Cheshire. In this part of the country, holes caused by melting ice in the last ice age became lakes. These gradually became covered over by a raft of bog, with a considerable depth of murky, peaty water below. Such places are known as* Schwingmoors *and they have a fascinating flora and fauna.*

PALMATE NEWT ON A MOUNTAIN BOG

A young palmate newt traversing the surface of a poolside bog on the lower slopes of Ben Eighe. Palmate newts can breed in almost any water and they do particularly well in acid and upland sites such as this. This individual was only about five centimetres long; it will grow considerably bigger.

ABBOT'S MOSS, CHESHIRE

When undisturbed, cranberry grows into sizeable hummocks which become covered with lovely pink flowers in June, followed later by berries in autumn.

EARLY MORNING IN A CHESHIRE BOG

*T*he photograph shows pines beginning to invade the floating bog surface of a 'Schwingmoor'. It was taken early in the morning to show the cobwebs. Usually the pines die when their roots break through the surface of the bog into the water which is below.

A NEW FOREST MARLPIT IN SPRING

*A*round the south of the New Forest, there is a series of old marlpits (opposite), dug out when marl (lime-rich clay) was a valuable commodity. Now they are beautiful ponds, rich in life, with bogbean, water plantain, water crowfoot, Hampshire purslane and other flowers visible.

BOG VEGETATION IN THE YORKSHIRE DALES

A close-up view (above) of the surface of a bog at Malham, showing the wonderful variety of leaf shape and colour to be found in such situations. The main species visible are bogbean (with leaves like broad beans), marsh cinquefoil and a carpet of bog moss.

BABY FROG ON FROG-BIT LEAVES

A young common frog just making its first forays into the open air, after ceasing to be a wholly aquatic tadpole. Appropriately enough, the leaves it is resting on are those of frog-bit and they are only a couple of centimetres in diameter. Within a few days, the emerging froglets will disperse from the pond, moving mainly at night.

RIVER RIBBLE, NORTH YORKSHIRE

*T*his dramatic sight, with a whole river as far as the eye can see filled with water crowfoot, was photographed in Ribblesdale, in the Yorkshire Dales. Chalk and limestone rivers, such as this, have a particular species of water crowfoot associated with them, and in certain years the floral display is spectacular. The extensive beds of crowfoot foliage are important areas for invertebrates and fish, for feeding and protection from predators (and anglers!). In many lowland chalk streams, the growth of aquatic plants is so luxuriant that the channel needs to be cut annually to prevent flooding.

BLANKET BOG BY MALHAM TARN

*I*n the more acid areas, around the beautiful Malham Tarn in the Yorkshire Dales National Park, where the peat has been raised above the alkaline water table, there is an extensive area of blanket bog (above). The dominant feature of the photograph is the seed heads of cotton grass.

MALHAM FEN AT DAWN

*A*round part of Malham Tarn, there is an extensive area of marginal fen, rich in plant life. One of the main channels running through the fen to the lake is shown here.

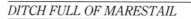

DITCH FULL OF MARESTAIL

*O*ne of the ditches running into Malham tarn, full of the
aquatic flowering plant, marestail. The low dawn sunlight
highlights the translucent side-branches of each plant.

RAGGED ROBIN IN A NORFOLK FEN

*S*hown is a mass of this beautiful flower growing in ungrazed fenland in a Norfolk Naturalists' Trust reserve in the fenlands of east Norfolk. It is a common plant in such situations, though rarely growing this luxuriantly.

FENLAND PLANTS, HAMPSHIRE

*T*he mixture of flowers that occurs in poor, rather acid, fens (below). The circular leaves are those of marsh pennywort, whilst the upright yellow flowers are of bog St John's wort.

SEDGE-RICH MEADOWS IN DYFED

*T*he photograph (opposite) shows part of a small nature reserve in Dyfed known as Rhos Fullbrook – the word Rhos means sedge-rich meadow locally. The plant in the foreground is red rattle and a number of other flushed grassland species, like marsh arrow grass, can be seen.

FRAMLINGHAM CASTLE, SUFFOLK

*B*elow the castle at Framlingham there is an old mere *surrounded by marshy vegetation. The photograph shows yellow flag iris growing in the marsh, with the misty outline of the castle beyond. The whole wetland area is a Suffolk Naturalists' Trust reserve.*

WATER LILIES IN A HIGHLAND LOCH

*W*hite water lilies close their flowers at night and the photograph (above) was taken late in the evening as the last rays of the Sun were disappearing. A large red damselfly is perched, probably in its roosting place for the night, on top of the closed flower.

NEW FOREST POND, HAMPSHIRE

A good example of a flowery New Forest pond, filled with water crowfoot, bog pondweed, pillwort and many other plants. All the open areas of the forest are grazed by ponies, which keep the edges of the ponds free of tall vegetation and even wade right into the ponds at times.

HEATHLAND
introduction by Simon King

The air is thick with the heady scent of bog myrtle. From somewhere deep in the coarse grasses, the ventriloqual clicking of a marsh grasshopper carries on a gentle breeze. A solitary pine, old and twisted, stands proud in a sea of heather like nature's flag of sovereignty.

Britain's lowland heaths have provided me with some of my most exciting and evocative memories. I have never felt that any other British habitat could boast such a unique character or such a delicate ecological balance. All the more unlikely, then, that most of our heathland was created by man. As our ancestors cleared away areas of woodland they allowed a new flora to gain a tenuous hold on the land. The gorses and heathers that are typical of heathland only survive with the help of some form of management. Browsing animals, cutting or burning prevents the invading species of tree and shrub from gaining the upper hand, and so maintains the open heath as we know it.

My time spent on heathland has tended to concentrate on the summer months. During the winter it lies sulking in the mists. Its wild visitors are few and far between, perhaps a hen harrier or a great grey shrike, both birds that appear and disappear like breath over the heather.

Only as the sun starts to warm up the year can the heath boast its full complement of natural marvels. The first adders slide out of their winter torpor to bask at the base of the fluff-covered crooks of unfurling bracken. High over the grassy bogland, even in the thickest mists of spring, the throbbing bleat of a drumming snipe can be heard proclaiming his territorial rights. By contrast, the rattling song of the Dartford warbler is dryness personified; it is as rough and scratchy as the gorse. These delicate, fidgety little birds are a taste of the Mediterranean; whenever I see one I think of olive groves and goatherds. Dusk on heathland brings with it still more specialities. The sun gone, the tall pines suddenly two-dimensional, their edges strikingly sharp and well defined against the violet glow in the west. A low mechanical churring noise rises up from the heather. The pitch increases then stops abruptly as the nightjar takes to the air. His floppy, buoyant flight is distinct against the western sky, blurred and ghostly against the east where he flicks up his wings and slaps them together high over his back, whip-cracking into the shadow of night.

I have to confess that my love of heathland has a lot to do with my love of a certain type of bird. It is the crowning glory of the heath and, though quite small, has a fiery spirit like the land it prefers. It is the hobby. There are few creatures more graceful or dashing than this raptor, who comes out of nowhere, scything low over the asphodel and sundew to snatch a dragonfly from the air. He bounces up from his strike and then glides slowly round, raising his prey to his beak and eating. It may sound silly to say this of a bird, but for a hobby, flying is a way of life!

It is sights and sounds like these that make Britain's heathland such a valuable natural asset. There is a black irony in the fact that a habitat which was created by man's development is now threatened by the very same thing. The pressure to reclaim what planners describe as 'waste-land' is enormous. With most of our heaths already lost to agricultural and housing projects there is precious little left to fight for. But I for one want my children to hear the gorse cracking in July's heat and smell the myrtle in the air. This delicate land has been pushed to the very limits of endurance. Its brittle character cannot withstand the pressure and will snap without our help and care.

Simon King

NEW FOREST, HAMPSHIRE

A typical late summer heathland scene, dominated by ling and bell heather.

Origins

Heathland is one of the most distinctive of all habitats, instantly recognizable and supporting a very characteristic range of plants and animals. The term may be applied to any fairly treeless habitat in which heather comprises a significant proportion of the vegetation, but in this chapter we shall restrict our consideration to lowland heaths, leaving upland moor to the following chapter.

Heathland is not a natural habitat but it is the form of vegetation which arises naturally on certain soils after woodland clearance and under the influence of grazing or burning. On the world scale it is very restricted, being confined to north-west Europe, southern South Africa, south-east Australia and a few oceanic islands. Vast tracts of heathland survived into the nineteenth century in France, Germany, Belgium, Denmark and Sweden, but nearly all of this was lost in not much more than one hundred years, mostly through afforestation and agriculture. In Britain only about 25% of the heathland present at the start of the nineteenth century survives today. Since the proportion lost on the continent has been even higher than this, there is a powerful international obligation on Britain to look after what remains. The warmer, more southerly parts of England are where heathland is best developed and this is where the characteristic heathland animals can be found.

Heather, or ling, is one of the dwarf shrubs which comprise the distinctive family of the Ericaceae. They are normally found on poor, acid soils where lack of minerals and nutrients prevents the establishment of other plants. Such conditions arise on porous sands and gravels from which all the soluble material is removed by the downward movement of rainwater. This material may be redeposited further down the soil profile, forming a dark layer half a metre or so below the surface. Such very distinctive soils are known as podsols. They lack the usual range of microscopic animals which live in vast numbers in the upper layers of fertile soils, recycling dead plant and animal matter and generally creating an amenable structure. Without micro-organisms to incorporate humus into a podsolized soil, dead plant material tends to gather as a thin brown or grey crust.

Heathlands usually have a wild, uncared-for appearance and tend to evoke various emotions. Some visitors are struck by the beauty of the flowering heather in late summer, others by the unspoilt, wilderness quality and the fascination of its wildlife. Yet other people, hopefully a small and declining number, condemn it as barren or even as an unsavoury and forbidding wasteland. This attitude is probably a direct legacy from bygone generations, for heathland was indeed the waste of the parish, the poorest soil, available to the commoners to supplement their meagre incomes by whatever legal means they could devise.

Most heathland succeeded the clearance of oak and birch woodland. Grazing prevented regeneration of cut stumps, and tree seedlings would not have survived long, for they would have been the most palatable material available to hard-pressed cattle, horses and goats. Grazing was probably the most significant influence in the development of heathland but no doubt fire played its part, for heather burns very readily and indeed the name ling is believed to have come from an Anglo-Saxon word for fire. Both burning and grazing would have exacerbated the impoverishment of the thin soils, gradually making conditions even more difficult for all but a few plants.

Male adder basking in the autumn light.

*GOLDEN-RINGED
DRAGONFLY ON
HAIR-MOSS*

*T**his dragonfly prefers
fast-flowing streams and
rivers in heathland and
moorland areas. It is one of
our longest and most striking
dragonflies.*

The Norman kings incorporated most of the larger areas of heathland into their royal forests, where hunting and cultivation were forbidden but local people had rights to graze stock and to collect wood and gravel. These traditions were later formalized into common rights pertaining to particular pieces of common land. The prohibition on cultivation was very important in maintaining the character of heathland, although much of it was lost through parliamentary Enclosure Acts at various dates up to the nineteenth century. The heathland which has survived to the present is only here by chance and as an incidental consequence of other forms of land use. Use for military training and common land status have both been very helpful by providing protection from the intensive pressures of agriculture, forestry and urban development. Unfortunately, as will be discussed later, sympathetic ownership and common rights have done little to reverse the disastrous effects of prolonged neglect of our heathland.

Plant communities

Heathland is typically a species-poor community and it can be composed entirely of heather with a few mosses and lichens. Usually, however, it is accompanied by bell heather with bright purple flowers, or cross-leaved heath

with clusters of pink flowers. The former grows on well-drained soils and the latter only where the ground is moist. They both flower earlier in the summer than heather, usefully extending the period when nectar is available to insects.

The heathers are often accompanied by gorse, which, being of the legume family, is able to assimilate nitrogen with the aid of nitrifying bacteria in its root nodules. There are three gorse species, all of them typically found on heathland. Bracken is present on many heaths, particularly where the soil is a little richer, and it can become dominant. Where there is a little shade or shelter to maintain humidity, bracken may develop into a pure stand, two metres high in the summer and almost impenetrable. It is unpalatable to stock, and after a fire or cutting, its extensive subterranean rhizome system enables it to send up fresh fronds with barely diminished vigour.

The commonest of the other higher plants to be found on dry heathland, other than the grasses, are tormentil, heath bedstraw, heath speedwell, sheep's sorrel, pill sedge, wood sage, petty whin and the parasitic dodder.

The Breckland area which straddles the Norfolk/Suffolk border is a strange mosaic of dry heathland and calcareous grassland, now heavily fragmented by agriculture and conifer plantations but still providing much to fascinate the ecologist and naturalist. The unusual plant communities developed under the influence of sheep and rabbit grazing on well-drained, wind-blown sands over chalk. The surface can be very acid where the sands are deep enough, and in such places the vegetation can be typical heather-dominated heathland. Elsewhere heather can be found in curious mixtures with species which require more base-rich soils.

Breckland has a 'continental' climate with hot, dry summers. Where summer temperatures are lower and moisture levels higher, a further range of heathland plants is able to thrive. These include two localized ericaceous plants, Dorset heath and Cornish heath. Both are particularly associated with heathland in the counties which give them their common names. Cornish heath is a tall, distinctive plant which grows on the Lizard peninsula, where the soil is mainly derived from serpentine limestone. This attractive, frost-free but windswept habitat contains many attractive plants.

Two habitats are recognized as intermediates between dry heath and mire. These are known as humid heath and wet heath, and they are best developed in central-south England, particularly Dorset, Hampshire and Surrey. Humid heath occurs where drainage is impeded, often on soils with a higher clay content, and wet heath occurs where the soils are waterlogged for part of the year. Neither is consistently wet enough to allow significant peat formation. Both humid and wet heath are dominated by a mixture of heather and cross-leaved heath. Humid heath is not well endowed with higher plants but has a good understorey of mosses and often an abundance of branched, crusty grey lichens. Wet heath, on the other hand, is characterized by a suite of flowering plants which make it one of the most rewarding of habitats for the botanist.

Animal life

THE LIZARD, CORNWALL

A mass of the beautiful hairy greenweed growing on the heathy cliff-top at Mullion Cove.

Several birds nest and feed in heathland, particularly where there is a scatter of gorse or other bushes. Skylark, meadow pipit, wren, linnet, whitethroat, willow warbler and grasshopper warbler can all be expected. There is only one bird species which in Britain is found exclusively on heathland, however, and that is the Dartford warbler. It occurs in a much wider range of habitats on the continent but in Britain it is confined to mature heaths in Dorset, Hampshire, the Isle of Wight and a small part of Surrey. It is one of the few warblers which do not trouble to migrate, choosing instead to spend the winter searching gorse and heather for insects and their eggs. It can continue feeding in gorse bushes underneath a canopy of snow but it is hardly surprising that the population can be decimated by hard winters. Sharing much the same habitat, but very much more numerous and extending to higher altitudes, is the stonechat, a chirpy extrovert in sharp contrast to the elusive Dartford warbler.

Where trees are present, even if only as a sparse scatter, the bird life can be a lot more varied and may include tree pipit, woodlark and nightjar. The latter's distinctive churring song, delivered between dusk and midnight and fluctuating in volume, is probably the most evocative of all heathland sounds.

The bird of prey most often associated with heathland is the hobby. It is not confined to this habitat but heathland is a favourite hunting ground. Here the hobbies take large numbers of dragonflies to supplement the regular diet of swallows and martins. Hobbies breed late in the year to take advantage of the new crop of young birds gathering to migrate.

Although they are seldom very evident, it is the 'herptiles', or reptiles and amphibians, which are the most numerous vertebrates in heathland and are most typically associated with the habitat. The adder and the common lizard can both be quite numerous, the latter comprising most of the food of the former. The smooth snake is confined in Britain to lowland heathland and the other two rare species, the sand lizard and natterjack toad, are found only on heathland or heathy sand dunes.

The sand lizard is the rarest and most endangered species. It requires warm, bare sand in which to lay its eggs, and many of the breeding sites have been lost as a result of recreation pressure, fire or invasion by birch and pine. Several of the remaining sites are on heathland in south Dorset, where they are threatened by development.

Insects

Nearly all the birds of heathland are insectivorous, and the herptiles eat either insects or each other. This happens because of the low numbers of small mammals, a phenomenon ultimately attributable to the soils and their lack of earthworms and other large invertebrates. Enormous numbers of insects have been recorded but a great many of them can occur in a variety of habitats, and many have drifted into heathland from habitats outside.

About forty insect species feed exclusively on heather or other ericaceous plants, not a very large number for a woody plant but a larger number will feed on heather in addition to other plants. A high proportion of the heathland invertebrate community turns out to be predatory, particularly the beetles, ants, bees, wasps and spiders. The bulk of their prey comprises moths, froghoppers and plant bugs, which can be present in large numbers. Grasshoppers are also plentiful on heathland, though usually more obvious to the ear than to the eye.

Two day-flying moths are very common, namely the silver-Y and the common heath. Rather less common but still occasionally seen in broad daylight are the wood tiger and the emperor moth. The latter is a very large moth with bright 'eyes' on the wings to deter avian predators.

A female sand wasp at its nest hole.

Most of the heathland moths fly only at night and they can be very numerous. Twenty-nine of the larger moth species have caterpillars which feed on heather, as do about twenty 'micromoths'.

There are only two butterflies which could legitimately be called heathland species, but many more which drift through or breed in a range of open habitats. The specialists are the grayling and silver-studded blue. Graylings are particularly associated with grassy heaths in which there is a lot of bare ground, their caterpillars feeding on fine grasses. The adults habitually alight on the barest ground, closing their wings and tilting towards the sun to control body temperature. The young caterpillars of the silver-studded blue feed on heather and cross-leaved heath. When they are about half-grown they are taken by ants and carried deep into their nests, where they complete their development and pupation.

Ants are normally the most numerous insects on heathland. This is why green woodpeckers, which are very partial to a meal of ants, are such frequent visitors to heathland. There are four common ant species, all of them living in complex subterranean communities and foraging over the ground or vegetation in search of seeds or insect prey.

The open ground is where one should look for the burrows of solitary bees and wasps. These illustrate a remarkable range of adaptations and specialized behaviour. Most species provision larders at the bottom of purpose-made tunnels. One or more insects or spiders are killed or paralysed and dragged down to the larder, whereupon the bee or wasp lays its eggs on the bodies so that the larvae are able to start eating as soon as they hatch.

Tiger beetles, of which there are four species in England, are another important component of the predatory insect fauna of heathland. The adults are fairly large, brightly coloured and armed with enormous jaws. They are very agile and pounce energetically on any unsuspecting prey such as flies or grasshoppers.

Open water is present in or adjacent to most heathland complexes, as little bog pools, peat cuttings, ditches or ponds. Such places provide particularly good habitat for dragonfly larvae, and the adult dragonflies hunt for small flying insects over the open heath or around trees. More than twenty species have been recorded from a few southern sites.

NEW FOREST, HAMPSHIRE

An autumn view, showing the way in which heath, bog and woodland blend easily into each other in the New Forest.

Management of heathland

Heathland is inherently unstable and will revert to woodland unless the ecological succession is inhibited by grazing, cutting, burning or removal of

invading trees. The exception to this is exposed western cliff-tops where the arresting force is provided by wind. Elsewhere, without intervention by man, trees will establish themselves and gradually shade out heather and gorse. Their deeper roots will tap into a greater volume of soil to harness a larger supply of nutrients, and their leaf litter will gradually enrich the soil. The rate of establishment of trees can be very slow where a dense cover of old heather or bracken inhibits seedlings, but such places seldom survive for long without being ravaged by fire.

Surrey and Sussex provide the most extensive examples of formerly open heathland which, in the absence of grazing for most of this century, has been heavily invaded by birch, pine, sallow and alder buckthorn. In nature reserves, and some commons managed by local authorities, extensive areas are now being prevented from reverting to woodland by programmes of scrub and tree removal, followed by treating cut stumps with herbicide.

A similar story can be told for the Suffolk Sandlings, an area up to sixteen kilometres wide along the Suffolk coast. In its heyday, when the land was used primarily as extensive sheep walk, there was close on 100 square kilometres of open heath. This has been reduced to only about twenty square kilometres, mainly through agricultural improvement, but an ambitious scheme is under way to reverse the trend.

The best example of grazed heathland in Britain is the New Forest in south-west Hampshire, where the rights of the commoners have been protected by Acts of Parliament and a system of pasturing ponies and cattle is still practised by local people. Other food resources, such as holly foliage and some of the plants in the bogs and streamside lawns, are vital to the health and survival of the animals, but all the heathland is subject to grazing throughout the year. Much of the heather is kept short, which reduces the diversity and abundance of insects, reptiles and small mammals.

The major influence on other heathland areas is recreation and amenity use. This can help to prevent scrub invasion but the consequence is usually localized erosion, accidental fires and disturbance of reptiles and ground-nesting birds by people and their dogs. Horseriding soon leads to erosion of the thin soils and development of bare sandy paths, which can gradually widen unless a degree of control is exercised. Even greater damage is caused by motorcycle scramblers, who have all but destroyed a number of heathland sites.

Pressures on heathland are therefore intense and likely to grow, so that the government-sponsored scheme to re-create heathland from arable farmland within the Breckland Environmentally Sensitive Area is greatly to be welcomed. Farmers are paid to deplete their land of nitrates and phosphates for two years before allowing natural regeneration of self-sown vegetation, followed by sheep grazing. It is hoped that experience here will show the way ahead for future enlargement of some of our old and very precious heathland fragments.

The other main hope for extending the area of heathland is to adopt a more draconian approach to the clearance of trees. Where heathland has been lost to birch or pine within the last fifty years there are still good prospects of much of the former wildlife returning if the trees are all felled, the stumps treated and the ground subsequently grazed. Clearly the future of Britain's heathland heritage will only be maintained when the problems are fully appreciated, the will to tackle them has developed and the government provides the necessary money.

HEATHER IN A SEA OF LICHENS

A gorgeous combination of a clump of ling in full flower, surrounded by a mass of Cladonia *lichen, on a heath in the Breckland area of Suffolk. Such lichen-rich heaths are relatively rare in the lowlands.*

MARSH FRITILLARY ON MEADOW THISTLE

*D*espite the names, the butterfly and flower (right) were photographed at a wet heath in Hampshire, managed by the Naturalists' Trust as a nature reserve. The larvae of marsh fritillaries feed on devil's bit scabious, so colonies tend to occur where this plant grows, that is on wet, grassy heaths, and on downland. Unfortunately it is a declining species.

MARSH CLUBMOSS ON WET HEATHLAND

A beautiful mixture of marsh clubmoss and cross-leaved heath on a damp southern heathland. The clubmoss is a non-flowering plant, more closely related to ferns than to flowers.

HEATHLAND ON AN AUTUMN MORNING

*H*eathland may appear to be almost devoid of life at times, but when you see a view like this, you realize the immense amount of life that is there. The early morning dew after a misty September night highlights every cobweb, and most of them are inhabited by spiders, all feeding on other invertebrates. The spiders themselves, along with other invertebrates, form the main food of the Dartford warbler, one of Britain's rarest birds.

The large almost-circular webs belong to orb-web spiders, such as the garden spider, whilst the others belong mainly to money spiders. This view was photographed very early in the morning in the New Forest, Hampshire.

149

PARASITIC DODDER ON GORSE AND HEATHER

*D*odder is a frequent inhabitant of heath and moor (opposite), where it grows as a total parasite on either heather or gorse. The pink trailing stems penetrate the host plants and then groups of pink flowers are produced in late summer.

PROSTRATE BROOM, KYNANCE COVE, CORNWALL

*T*his gorgeous mass of flowers is produced by the bushes of a prostrate form of broom, found only in a few heathy coastal areas in south-west Britain. The bushes are at most fifteen centimetres high.

A CORNISH HEATHLAND MIXTURE

A lovely combination of white-flowered Cornish heath and bell heather (below) that could only be found in Cornwall. The mild, damp climate and particular soil of southern Cornwall is ideally suited to the growth of heathers.

GREEN TIGER BEETLE ON SANDY HEATHLAND

*T*he dramatically coloured green tiger beetle is a common species on sandy heathlands, avidly preying on other insects. The larvae live in burrows in the sand, grabbing anything unfortunate enough to come close to them.

CORNISH HEATH, THE LIZARD, CORNWALL

A beautiful clump of the rare Cornish heath, growing above Mullion Cove, Cornwall. Within Britain, this plant is virtually confined to the heaths on serpentine rock in this area, though it is surprisingly abundant where it does occur.

SPRING SANDWORT, THE LIZARD, CORNWALL

The beautiful white-flowered clumps of spring sandwort appear on bare stony ground on heaths on The Lizard, though elsewhere they may grow on limestone, or even on the spoil from leadmines.

SAND LIZARD

A close view of a female sand lizard on heathland in Dorset. Sand lizards are now rare and confined to just a few areas in Dorset, Hampshire and north-west England.

LICHEN HEATH IN THE BRECKLANDS

P arts of the strange Breckland area support an especially lichen-rich heathland. This attractive clump of Cladonia *lichen* (below)*, with its striking, red, fruiting bodies, was growing at Lakenheath Warren, Suffolk.*

FOX MOTH CATERPILLAR

*T*he striking furry caterpillar of the fox moth (above) is a
common sight on many heaths and moors. It is seen here
on a lichen-rich moor in the Spey Valley, Scotland, after heavy
rain in September, just before it goes to pupate.

MARSH GENTIAN ON A DORSET HEATH

*T*he rare and beautiful marsh gentian grows on wet heaths
in various parts of Britain, often occupying the dividing
zone between heath and bog. It is seen here growing on
Purbeck, with cross-leaved heath (with the grey leaves) and
ling, in flower, in late September.

155

GRAYLING BUTTERFLY VISITING LING FLOWERS

*T*he grayling is one of our few specialist heathland butterflies, though it also occurs on similar habitats on the coast. It is a declining species, which has disappeared from many former haunts.

MOORLAND FLOWERS ON DARTMOOR

*T*he combination of colours when heathers and western gorse come into flower together in late summer is beautiful. The main flowers in this scene (opposite) photographed on Haytor, are western gorse, bell heather, and the pale-coloured ling.

SOUTHERN HAWKER DRAGONFLY ON HEATHER

*T*his female southern hawker has perched on a bell heather bush to bask in the sun and to eat her insect prey. This photograph was taken in high summer in the New Forest, where this species breeds in bogs. However, it often feeds over heathland.

DARTMOOR PONIES ON MOORLAND

*T*he high moorlands of Dartmoor are midway between lowland heaths and uplands, though they share most plants and animals with heathland. In this late summer view, on the slopes of Haytor, the main species visible are ling, bell heather, western gorse, bracken, and bristle bent (the brownish grass spikes). Ponies graze the moorland extensively, under common grazing rights, helping to keep the moorland open. Lower parts of the moor would gradually succeed to woodland under the present climate, if left ungrazed.

159

UPLANDS
introduction by Robert Hardy

If you drive northward on the A1 motorway from Wetherby, the rich Yorkshire landscape rolls away on either side, woodland, ploughland and pasture, compared with the constriction and enclosure, the overbuilding and crowding of the South East, offering space and size, freeing the spirit.

Gradually, as you drive on, there appears a lifted smudge on the horizon, like an island seen in the distance from a ship at sea; or is it cloud? Gradually it reveals itself as the first view of uplands, of the Dales.

If you drive from the centre of England westward into the borderland and Wales, or south west towards Exmoor and Dartmoor, or northward from Yorkshire through the Scottish lowlands, on upward to the Highlands, to the Islands, that awesome first glimpse of high country catches the eye and the mind and sets the imagination spinning. Heather, rock, grasses blowing, leaning stunted trees, sheep in the wind, crag, waterfall, hill and mountain. Those high wild spaces, yearned for by so many people, are today threatened by the demands and the ignorance of what we call civilization.

Most of us in Britain want the wild places to remain wild. Some of us want to walk in them, some even climb, or ride in them; most are content to drive through them picnicking on the way, and for some it is enough to see pictures of them in magazines or on television, but almost all would be deeply shocked to feel our wilderness was under threat. Up in the wilds today, not only is there the sudden tearing roar of jets, sweeping the ancient contours, there is the concussion of stone-blasting, the vast scars of quarrying, the striding concrete and spreading water of hydro-electric schemes. There is the silent dark march of conifer forests, blanketing the hills and valleys, forbidding many wild creatures, poisoning the ground and the streams, rank on endless rank of suffocating sameness. Many upland owners have gone into quick-grow, quick-harvest forestry to increase their income from a tough and poor holding. Lowland farmers, squeezed by the milk and cereal quotas ordained in Brussels, move into sheep and spread upwards into the high lands, eroding the very ground they feed on, pushing the hill farmer and the crofter to the very edge of survival. But crofting and hill farming are the very means, the benign means, of preserving the uplands. Left desolate they would become inaccessible except to the giant machines that dig out the wild growth to plant the conifer, or scour the moorlands for stone, for water, for energy.

The tourist in the summer may realize little of the danger, and indeed it is the tourist who is bringing money to the wild lands, and so helping to support those who tear a living from the harsh moor and hills; though as he basks in his achievement, the tourist himself in all innocence tramps the upland trails until the surfaces begin to crumble.

The sporting uplander who organizes his moors for game, and lets his shooting, brings in money which preserves some of the wilderness; he drains bogs, kills bracken, encourages heather, and just as the crofter, fears the growing numbers of sheep, and the overgrazing. The crofter and the hill farmer will no longer bear the miserable living conditions of their forebears; they want access to their farms by road, and to the shops from their farms. They want telephones, television, the things that a vast majority of the nation now takes for granted, but their return on their land is frighteningly small: in the Highlands something like fifty pence an hour of labour per acre. Yet they are the custodians of much that is most precious in our ecology.

We must realize quickly that if we wish our wildlands to survive, for our joy, and for our children's, then we must subsidize those who labour to preserve them, and we must make our Government do as we wish.

Robert Hardy

12 : XII : 89

MULL, WEST SCOTLAND

A beautiful waterfall in the mountains of Mull, taken in autumn with the bracken just turning.

The upland habitat

*A*way from the better-known areas around the Spey Valley, there are vast areas of peaceful heather moorland and tundra in the Cairngorms. This photograph, taken on the eastern slopes of the Cairngorms, also shows junipers and a single birch.

Plants and animals which live at high altitude must be able to tolerate low temperatures, high wind, heavy and prolonged rain, constant humidity and long periods of snow cover. Obviously these factors become more extreme at higher altitude. The climate and the fact that most of the higher ground in the British Isles is underlain by acid, base-poor rocks conspire to prevent the development of deep, fertile soils. Upland vegetation is dominated, therefore, by hardy plants which are efficient at making the most of low levels of available nutrients. They are essentially slow-growing, long-lived perennial plants.

These same climatic and soil factors have also imposed major restrictions on agriculture, so that grazing by tough hill sheep is the only option available

to those wishing to farm the land. The animals need to forage over a large area and must be capable of surviving with a minimum of care. The limitations on farming have enabled enormous areas of semi-natural vegetation to survive. The plant communities of vast, upland tracts vary not as a result of man's activities but in response to aspect, altitude and rock type. This is in stark contrast to lowland Britain, where semi-natural vegetation occurs as a scatter of islands in a sea of intensively managed farmland. The uplands represent the last great wilderness, where the hand of man is often hard to discern and where the species most intolerant of man find their refuge.

The only place in Britain where the natural tree line is discernible is in the Cairngorms, at an altitude of 610–640 metres (2000–2100 feet). If semi-natural woodland was allowed to re-establish itself elsewhere, it would become apparent that trees are capable of growing on a very high proportion of our hill and mountain country. With today's climate the natural woodland cover of most of the uplands is birch, pine and rowan, but the original wildwood was very different.

Pollen evidence suggests that unbroken forest with oak, elm and hazel covered much of the uplands until about 3000 BC. A sharp decline was brought about at this time by a combination of soil acidification and the actions of Neolithic farmers. They cleared the woodland to create open ground for their cattle and cut branches for fodder. The rate of clearance accelerated enormously during the Iron Age and pastoral farming was introduced to most of the uplands. A wetter, cooler period during the first millennium BC encouraged marsh plants and bog mosses and resulted in a great expansion of blanket bog. Much of the remaining woodland was engulfed by a gradual accumulation of peat. Woodland clearance continued spasmodically, slowly eating into the remnants on steeper slopes and the least fertile soils. The lowest ebb came in the seventeenth century, after which some areas of new woodland were established, mostly by planting but also by natural regeneration in a few areas. The last fragments of ancient, semi-natural, broadleaved woodland survive in the uplands only in the least accessible places remote from access roads and on steep, rocky slopes which would have been difficult to clear and where grazing pressure was very light. Fortunately, much of the Caledonian pinewood area in the central Highlands of Scotland was never cleared, allowing the survival of many relic plant and insect species which may have been there for more than 10,000 years.

The plant communities of open moorland and mountain are partly determined by climate. It is important to remember, however, that temperatures drop and rainfall increases not only with altitude but also with latitude. Vegetation transitions one can see when climbing a mountain are repeated when travelling northwards through Britain. The climatic conditions prevailing at high altitude in England or Wales can be found at a progressively lower altitude up to the north of Scotland. For this reason it is not possible to classify vegetation on the basis of altitude alone.

Plant communities

The richest upland plant communities are to be found where the vegetation has been altered least by the removal of the forest cover. Such areas occur where grazing is relatively light and burning is, at most, infrequent. Very large areas are not like this, however, and the community is relatively species-

*T*his is one of our most beautiful wild flowers. This particularly attractive clump was growing on a wet mountainside on the island of Mull, west Scotland, where it is common.

poor, uniform and lacking in many botanical surprises. Variety is generally provided by local variations in geology producing more base-rich conditions and by cliff ledges and screes where grazing animals fear to tread.

The plant best suited to the soils and climate of upland Britain is undoubtedly heather, or ling. Huge areas of rolling moorland and blanket bog are still dominated by this tough dwarf shrub which happily tolerates frost, high wind, prolonged snow cover, occasional burning and moderate levels of grazing. The plant is a very welcome asset, for it is a valuable species for wildlife and a vital component of the habitat of those two very significant quarry species, the red grouse and the red deer.

A high proportion of open moorland is actually a grass/heath mixture, in which the most constant grass species are both very fine-leaved, namely common bent and sheep's-fescue. Heather is often present in mixture with bilberry, whose stiff green branches, glossy leaves and occasional purple fruits add texture and interest to the turf. Management of grouse moors has maintained an enormous area of such dwarf shrub vegetation in Scotland, and at higher altitudes heather moorland mixed with patches of thin, upland grassland is used primarily for stalking red deer.

As one climbs up through hills dominated by grasses, heather or bilberry, the first truly upland plant to appear will probably be crowberry. This may soon be followed by cowberry and, particularly in Scotland, bearberry and bog bilberry. Such communities dominated by dwarf shrubs are often very similar to the vegetation under the rather open canopy of the native pinewoods.

With increasing altitude, mosses, ferns, particularly mountain fern and parsley fern, and those peculiar fern allies the clubmosses become more commonplace. In truly montane conditions the physical forces of wind and rain are more severe, causing erosion and permanently open bare ground. Lichens and mosses provide the majority of the species and can be dominant at high altitude. Where temperature and exposure permit, the ground is usually grass-covered but even sheep's-fescue finally gives up, leaving the ground for the very specialized stiff sedge and three-leaved rush. The best place to look for high mountain flowers, such as alpine lady's-mantle, alpine pearlwort and various saxifrages, is where they can find a little shelter from the wind, which is also where the snow lies deepest. Several attractive species are capable of slow growth under snow and of flowering shortly after the early summer sunshine has lifted the white mantle.

Peat formation becomes increasingly significant at higher altitude and latitude, with extensive blanket bogs becoming more common and finally truly blanketing the vast Flow Country of Caithness and Sutherland. All upland bogs support a variety of specialized plants whose local distribution is the result of prolonged interplay of natural ecological factors. Cloudberry, a relative of brambles but with single flowers, picks out the better-drained spots within high-altitude peat bogs; cranberry grows on tight hummocks of *Sphagnum*, while bog rosemary is confined to the most acid and waterlogged situations, particularly in the Pennines and Scottish Borders.

Geology and plants

In addition to climate, wetness and grazing pressure, rock type exerts a profound influence over the vegetation. Most of the uplands are composed of hard, acidic rocks of volcanic origin, very deficient in bases such as calcium and magnesium. Where this is not the case, the flora is very much richer, with many attractive flowers typical of arctic or alpine habitats. The Pennines contain extensive areas of carboniferous limestone, particularly in Derbyshire and Yorkshire, and smaller areas of base-rich rock occur in Snowdonia, the Brecon Beacons, the Lake District and the Mendips. Scotland is relatively poor in base-rich upland vegetation but where it does occur, such as in the Breadalbane range, the montane flora is of very great botanical interest.

At lower levels, upland base-rich vegetation and limestone grassland share an indefinable common boundary. Derbyshire dales such as Dove Dale and Lathkill Dale provide magnificent examples of herb-rich vegetation which could be regarded as either upland or lowland. Typical limestone grassland species such as kidney vetch and quaking grass overlap up the slope with species more typical of open woody hillsides, limestone crags and screes. These rocky habitats support a very rich community with several large and distinctive species such as melancholy thistle, field garlic, limestone fern, stone bramble and Jacob's-ladder.

On the limestone fells of the north Pennines a distinctive grass called blue moor-grass can achieve a high level of dominance. The strictly upland distribution of this species in Britain is very curious in view of its lowland distribution on the continent, growing on chalk up to the coast of northern France.

Red grouse – one of the most typical birds of the upland moors and fells.

In regions of high rainfall the limestone may have been eroded in a spectacular manner, creating deep river gorges, swallow holes and caves. In some areas the limestone has been eroded into relatively flat, smooth blocks separated by fissures. This limestone-pavement habitat is of great botanical interest, with many uncommon species and improbable communities of plants which would normally never be seen together. By growing in the fissures, or grykes, plants can find the same physical conditions of light and humidity that they would normally encounter in woodland. The most interesting regions for limestone pavement are in Yorkshire, Lancashire, Cumbria and some small areas in County Fermanagh.

One of the most exceptional areas of upland vegetation in Britain, which has an extraordinary concentration of rare plant species, is Upper Teesdale, straddling the border between North Yorkshire and Durham. The survival of the unique flora is believed to be attributable to the unusual geological conditions, where the structure of the limestone was altered by an intrusion of igneous rock to produce granular material aptly known as sugar limestone. Much of the area is believed to have remained continuously free of trees since before the last glaciation, providing a refuge for alpine plants of base-rich rocks.

It is in only a few places in the Scottish Highlands, however, where the rocks are rich in soluble bases, that one can appreciate Britain's finest displays of alpine vegetation. On Ben Lawers and Ben Lui in the Breadalbane mountain range on the borders of Argyll and Perthshire, rocks known as the Dalradian schists outcrop at an altitude of about 1000 metres (3280 feet). They are sufficiently base-rich to support no less than 60% of Britain's mountain flowers. Cliffs and rock ledges are the most favourable situations, offering freedom from grazing, better drainage and reduced competition, but even relatively flat ground can be very species-rich.

Predators and prey

The range of birds and mammals in mountain and moorland country is very different from that in lowland farmland. Not only is the climate more demanding and the soils less productive, but the lack of woodland, hedgerows and rank, ungrazed vegetation obviously exerts a strong influence on availability of food and shelter. For birds and mammals the quantity and diversity of possible food items, be they fruits, seeds, shoots, invertebrate or vertebrate animals, are very much more limited. These limitations militate against omnivores and generalists and favour specialist predators. Many predators have also been forced to shun the populated parts of the country in favour of the most remote, inaccessible corners of the land. They all had much wider breeding ranges in the past but were driven back, in some cases to extinction, by our intolerant ancestors.

Increasing altitude and latitude see a gradual reduction in small mammals, particularly wood mice, bank voles, water voles and shrews. Rabbits and short-tailed voles are present up to quite high altitudes but at a much lower density than in lowland grassland.

The qualities required for a successful upland predator are therefore the ability to withstand a harsh climate, to hunt over a very large area without using much energy, to be quick and efficient when it comes to the kill and to make the most of every meal and thereby feed less frequently. In addition,

Although the dunlin is most often seen wintering along our coasts, it breeds amongst grassy tussocks in upland moors and bogs.

*The dramatically steep
and eroded slopes of the
Ben Eighe massif, seen from
the east. The National Nature
Reserve here covers a huge
area of some of the wildest
and most exciting country in
Britain.*

resourcefulness and opportunism are invaluable qualities in any predator. Every predator hunts over more than one kind of terrain, and the greater the variety, the greater the possible range of prey. Moving to higher altitude usually reduces the variety of terrain as well as the numbers and range of food items. The highest-altitude predators are therefore the most specialized. If one were to place the main avian predators on a gradient of increasing adaptation to upland conditions, the sequence would probably be buzzard, short-eared owl, hen harrier, peregrine, merlin and golden eagle.

To complete the picture, ravens are typically upland birds but they should not strictly be regarded as predators as they depend heavily on carrion, supplemented by eggs and chicks. Another predator, the osprey, is associated with freshwater lochs in the Scottish Highlands. After an absence of forty-three years this magnificent bird bred successfully in 1959, under the protection of the Royal Society for the Protection of Birds. The species continues to expand its breeding range, nesting in trees sometimes as much as three or four kilometres from the nearest feeding site. The largest of all the British predatory birds is the white-tailed or sea eagle. This aristocrat is partial to sickly or dead fish and therefore frequents the shores of sea or freshwater lochs. It was reintroduced to the Western Isles of Scotland by the Nature Conservancy Council in the 1980s, and an increase in range and population is eagerly awaited.

The buzzard is often seen soaring impassively over open moorland but it nests in trees and is perfectly well adapted to life in the lowlands. It is mainly persecution, chiefly by gamekeepers, which restricts the species to a western and upland distribution. Buzzards supplement their main diet of voles and rabbits with occasional carrion, particularly lambs, but better farming practices are reducing this supply.

Short-eared owls breed in more remote, higher-altitude moorland than buzzards but they will also nest in sand dunes or grazing marshland. They nest on the ground and their main need seems to be freedom from human disturbance, a requirement increasingly difficult to meet in lowland Britain.

Hen harriers are delightfully elegant birds of prey, with unmistakably long wings and tail. They are frequent visitors to lowland England on passage and during the winter. When spring comes, however, they return to their upland haunts to defend a territory, establish a firm bond with a mate (very probably the same individual as the previous year) and cement this relationship with acrobatic aerial displays including passing food from one bird to the other, followed by nest construction. Hen harriers feed on small mammals and small birds, both of which are more numerous in the first few years of a conifer plantation, after the sheep have been fenced out.

RED DEER, ARGYLL

This red deer stag has its antlers in velvet. When the velvety skin is shed in late summer the antlers harden, heralding a new rutting season. The antlers are cast each year and a new pair grows from the bony pedicels.

Both the peregrine and the merlin feed almost exclusively on birds, which they catch in flight. The peregrine is the largest of the British falcons and the merlin the smallest. A proportion of British peregrines has always nested on sea cliffs, however, and increasingly, as they continue to recover from the 1960s crash which was caused by pesticides such as DDT and dieldrin, they are extending their breeding area into lowland counties.

Merlins feed entirely on small birds such as meadow pipits and breed in open moorland and extensive blanket bog. The nest is made on the ground, usually in fairly tall vegetation such as long heather. They are very scarce, therefore, on heavily grazed fells and well-managed grouse moors. Frequent burning and human disturbance are clearly very unwelcome to these discerning birds, whose numbers have declined in recent years.

Few people can watch a golden eagle without some feelings of awe. It must be the most majestic and magnificent of all British birds and the Scottish population of around 300 pairs is of great international importance, for they have been declining everywhere on the continent of Europe. Golden eagles require a territory of up to sixty square kilometres for hunting and that area must be subject to minimal disturbances, for they are very sensitive, particularly in spring when they reoccupy the traditional nest site.

The high-level relative of the red grouse, the ptarmigan, which turns white in winter to avoid standing out against the snow, is an important prey item for the golden eagle. So too is that extraordinary hardy animal, the mountain, or blue, hare. Sheep carrion is quite important to the survival of the Scottish eagles, but the killing of a healthy lamb or fawn is said to be a rare event.

In addition to the predators several waders, such as the golden plover and dunlin, nest amongst the grass tussocks of the blanket bogs and upland moors.

The Flow Country

In the far north of Scotland, in the Flow Country of Caithness and Sutherland, where the colder, wetter climate allows blanket bog to descend to sea level, a vast expanse of near-natural vegetation represents the last truly great wilderness in the British Isles. It is very likely that most of this area has remained free of trees since before the last ice age. It is a fine example of boreal vegetation, similar to vast tracts of northern Norway and Sweden but with important Atlantic features not represented there. This is not the place to document the riches of the area but no account of the British uplands would be complete without mentioning something of this wilderness and its extraordinary breeding bird community. The statistics speak for themselves. The Flow Country supports no less than 18% of Britain's breeding population of golden plover, 20% of the black-throated diver, 39% of the dunlin, 39% of the common scoter and no less than 66% of the greenshank. The tragedy is that, for reasons which have more to do with grants and taxation than ecology, all the power of modern technology has been used to transform the area into plantations of exotic conifer. The difficulty of getting about the area and demonstrating its unique value has proved a major obstacle in convincing the nation's decision-makers of the importance of these issues. The British uplands are a priceless asset. The most northerly extremity of that great legacy needs to be protected as vigorously as our great cathedrals, the Cairngorms or Wordsworth's beloved Lake District.

LINGMOOR FELL, CUMBRIA

*R*owans in fruit light up in a shaft of autumn sunshine. Surrounding the rowans are masses of juniper bushes or trees, many of them very old, forming an extensive low open woodland filling much of the valley. Beyond, in the shadow of the clouds, lie Horse Crags and the Wrynose Pass. The foreground is made up of damp grassland, partly boggy and partly drier with anthills.

171

BILBERRY, CAIRNGORMS

*T*he striking red autumn foliage of bilberry (above)
contrasts with the grey and green lichens on a rock in an
upland birchwood in the Spey Valley.

BEN EIGHE, NORTH-WEST SCOTLAND

A lone Scots Pine (opposite) marks the present upper limit
of Caledonian pine forest on Ben Eighe, at about 300
metres (1000 feet). Once, the forest extended much higher up
the mountains, but grazing and burning reduced its extent.
Now, efforts are being made to allow it to grow back to its
natural limits by excluding grazing.

BEN EIGH NATIONAL NATURE RESERVE

A *female ptarmigan in her natural high mountain habitat, the mountain areas of Highland Scotland, looking north from Ben Eighe (left). Ptarmigan rear their young in the highest mountain areas and remain high for the whole year. In winter, they become white and develop a thicker more protective plumage, with extra feathers on the legs.*

FEMALE PTARMIGAN

A *closer view of this beautiful bird, one of our few specialist high mountain birds.*

MOUNTAIN PANSIES

*T*his species is a feature of upland pastures in limestone areas. This beautiful mass of yellow and purple flowers is growing in a hay meadow in upper Teesdale. In some areas, the flowers are predominantly blue, in others they are predominantly yellow, whilst some places have a mixture.

FALLEN ROWAN BERRIES

*L*ate September gales in the Spey valley had shaken berries, leaves and whole branches of rowans onto the ground below. The combination of their autumn colours with the purple of heather and the bright green of bog moss was irresistible.

LOCH SPELVE, WEST SCOTLAND

A rowan, or mountain ash, deformed by the prevailing wind, on the shore of Loch Spelve, a sea-loch on Mull. The clarity of the air and brightness of the colours after overnight heavy rain was startling.

177

MAIDENHAIR SPLEENWORT FERN

This example is growing between whin sill blocks below Cronkley Fell, Upper Teesdale. The hard rock of this volcanic material supports a surprising array of plant life on cliffs, quarries and walls in the dale.

PEAK DISTRICT, DERBYSHIRE

The Carboniferous limestone outcrops of the southern part of the Peak District make superb wild rock-gardens, with numerous rare and attractive plants, including bloody cranesbill and rock-rose. This photograph was taken at Cressbrookdale, within the Peak District National Nature Reserve.

HOARY ROCKROSE

Various colour forms of this rare rockrose growing on the strange 'sugar limestone' at about 500 metres (1650 feet) in Upper Teesdale, County Durham. Strictly speaking the rock is a marble, as it has been metamorphosed from the original limestone by the great heat of a volcanic intrusion. The resulting easily eroded soil supports more rare plants than almost anywhere else in Britain.

179

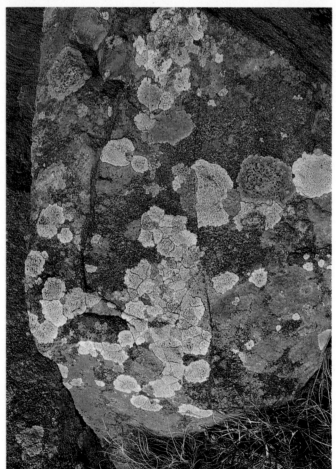

LICHENS IN THE PENNINES

These lichens are growing on whin sill rock in Upper Teesdale, County Durham. In general, mountain areas are good for lichens, because the air is clean and unpolluted, and other plants do not grow strongly enough to out-compete them here.

BEN EIGHE NATIONAL NATURE RESERVE

*T*he slopes of Creag Dubh and Ruadh-stac-beag, above Loch Maree in western Scotland (opposite), epitomize wild mountain scenery as it occurs in Britain. Only relatively few plants and animals survive in these inhospitable conditions.

ALPINE FORGET-ME-NOT

*T*his is one of the rarest and most attractive of our alpine flowers. It is growing here on a ledge on Ben Lawers, Tayside, one of only two areas in which it is found in Britain.

CAIRNGORMS NATIONAL NATURE RESERVE

*E*ven in June snow still lingers in sheltered high areas of the Cairngorms (below). This photograph was taken on the top of the granitic plateau at 1200 metres (4000 feet).

BEN LAWERS, TAYSIDE

*T*he rock ledges on the mica schist around the higher parts
of Ben Lawers are the best natural rock gardens in
Britain, with masses of rare and attractive flowers, including
alpine forget-me-not, several saxifrages and snow gentian.

HIGH MOUNTAIN FLORA

A high altitude mixture
(right) of fir clubmoss (a
close relative of the ferns),
various rock-living lichens
and starry saxifrage growing
close to the top of Ben
Lawers, Tayside.

HIGH MOUNTAIN FLORA

*A*t the highest levels on
Scottish mountains, the
plant life becomes dwarfed;
this picture shows lichens and
a mountain willow only a few
centimetres high. This
photograph was taken close
to the summit of Ben Lawers,
Tayside, at about 1000
metres (3300 feet).

MOSSY MOUNTAIN STREAM

*T*his mountain rill about 600 metres (2000 feet) up on the slopes of Ruadh-stac-Beag in Ross and Cromarty, within the Ben Eighe National Nature Reserve. The wet area is almost totally dominated by moss growth of unexpected colours.

SGURR BAN, NORTH-WEST SCOTLAND

A glacial corrie tarn below the cliffs of Sgurr Ban, in the Ben Eighe National Nature Reserve. Such tarns are relics of the previous ice-ages in Britain, though the glaciers that formed them no longer exist.

CRAIGELLACHIE BIRCH WOOD SPEY VALLEY

*T*his wood (below), above Aviemore, is one of the best examples of an upland birch wood, beautiful at any time of year. The open nature of the canopy is typical of natural northern woods, grazed by deer or domestic animals.

LIMESTONE PAVEMENT

*T*hese are strange places, with mixtures of woodland and grassland plants growing in cracks in massive block limestone. The pavement-like blocks are called clints, and the fissures are grykes (opposite). In the British Isles, such pavement areas occur particularly in the Craven area of North Yorkshire, around Morecambe Bay, and in the Burren of western Ireland, always on Carboniferous limestone. The photograph above shows young fronds of hart's tongue fern unfurling in a gryke, and the one to the left shows a beautiful mixture of bloody cranesbill and bird's foot trefoil at Scar Close, North Yorkshire.

LITTLE LANGDALE TARN, LAKE DISTRICT

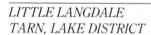

*S*omehow, this view *S*encapsulates much of what the Lake District has to offer – an unspoilt, fen-fringed tarn, grazed pastures and the mountains beyond, with woodlands and trees scattered about. Typically, it had just rained, and the sun only appeared for a few minutes on a windy autumn day, at a time when southern England was still basking in settled Mediterranean weather! In the middle distance, it is possible to see how the stone-walled fields have crept up the mountainside, ceasing where the terrain and climate becomes too inhospitable, leaving the higher pastures unimproved and unenclosed.

kestrel 141
kettle-holes 108
kingfisher 106
kite, red 9
kittiwake 19
knapweed 83
Knapwell Wood, Cambridgeshire 75
knot 15
Kynance Cove, Cornwall 151

lacewing 53
lady's-mantle, alpine 165
lady's smock 83
lagoons 17
Lake District 108, 165
Lakenheath Warren, Suffolk 154
lakes 107, 108
Lancashire 15, 166
Langdon Beck, Upper Teesdale 119
Langstone Harbour 15
lapwing 84, 101
lark, shore 20
Lathkill Dale 165
leech 110
leys 80, 145
lichen 8, 49, 51, 52, 57, 61, 62, 72, 80,
   100, 139, 141, 155, 165, 172, 180,
   183
   bark-living 49
   Cladonia 146, 154
lime, small-leaved 8, 61
limestone 16, 18, 29, 41, 57, 74, 80,
   94, 98, 109, 153, 165, 166, 175
   carboniferous 80, 95, 165, 179, 186
   magnesium 80
   serpentine 141
   sugar 166, 179
limpet, blue-rayed 16
Lincolnshire 82
ling 136, 138, 146, 155, 156, 159, 164
Lingmoor Fell, Cumbria 171
linnet 141
Little Langdale Tarn 188
Littondale, Yorkshire Dales 76
liverwort 49, 61, 62, 112
lizard, common 142
   sand 9, 142, 154
Lizard peninsula 18, 36, 37, 141, 153
lobelia, water 120
Loch an Eileann 117
Lochnagar, mountains of 108–9
lochs, sea 15, 20, 21, 30, 33, 42
Lower Kingcombe, Dorset 72
lowlands 9, 48, 50, 55, 79, 110, 111,
   138, 159, 163, 166
Lundy Island 16, 28
lungwort, narrow-leaved 55

male-fern 90
Malham 80, 126
Malham Tarn 112, 130
Mallachie, Loch 114
mallow, tree 18
mammals 55, 142, 145, 166
   see also individual species
Maree, Loch 66, 110
marestail 131
marigold, corn 96
   marsh 82
Mark Ash, New Forest 71
marlpits 126
marram 16
marsh 16, 109, 117
Marwick Head 18
mat-grass 100
mayflies 106, 109
meadows 9, 72, 80–3, 93, 100, 132
   hay 7, 76, 78, 80, 86, 90, 101, 175
   wet 81, 82
meadowsweet 81, 119
Mendips 165
meres 108, 109
merganser, red-breasted 108
merlin 9, 167, 169
micromoths 143
Midlands 5, 79, 83
milkwort 80
   chalk 8
Miller's Dale, Derbyshire 98
Millersdale, Peak District National
   Park 119
millipedes 53, 142
minnow 107
Minsmere, Suffolk 111
mire 112, 141
mole 54

molluscs, bivalve 15
Monewden Meadows, Suffolk 88
moor-grass, blue 165
moorland 9, 55, 112, 138, 151, 156,
   159, 162–9
   see also heathlands, uplands
Moray Firth 14, 49
Morecambe Bay 15, 186
mosquitoes 106
moss 17, 50, 61, 62, 80, 108, 110, 112,
   113, 121, 139, 141, 165, 185
   bog- 110, 123, 126, 163, 177
   hair- 139
   Sphagnum 17, 110, 112, 165
moths 38, 54, 84, 142, 143, 155
   see also individual species
mountain ash *see* rowan
mouse, wood 54, 166
mudflats 15, 16, 21
Mull 42, 90, 160, 164
Mullion Cove, Cornwall 37, 141, 153
musk, monkey 119

Nairn, Moray Firth 14
National Trust 8
Nature Conservancy Council 8, 167
nature reserves 7, 8, 9, 85
Nene Washes 82
New Forest 8, 51, 57, 74, 85, 112,
   126, 135, 136, 145
newt 106
   palmate 124
nightingale 54
nightjar 142
Norfolk 82, 109, 112, 113, 132, 141,
   154
North Meadow National Nature
   Reserve, Wiltshire 81
Northend, Avon 69
Northern Ireland 16, 19, 55, 82, 83,
   112
Nottingham 80
Noup Cliffs, Orkney 18

oak 8, 51, 56, 57, 138, 163
Oak Mere 108
oak-woods 49
oat-grass, meadow 80
orchid, burnt 8
   early marsh 113
   early purple 50
   fragrant 113
   green-winged 83, 103
   lax-flowered 93
   marsh 17, 39
   monkey 9
   southern marsh 113
   spotted 39
Orford Ness 17
osprey 106, 167
otter 9, 20, 43, 106
Ouse Washes 82
owl, barn 9
   short-eared 167, 168
   tawny 55
Oxfordshire 113
oxlip 49, 68, 75
oystercatcher 18
oysterplant 17

pansy, mountain 175
Papa Westray 18
partridge, grey 84
Peak District 179
pearlwort, alpine 165
peat 109, 112, 113, 144, 163, 165
Pembrokeshire 16, 18
Pennines 163, 165
pennywort, marsh 113, 132
peregrine 9, 167, 169
Perthshire 166
Pevensey Levels 82
Pholiota, Shaggy 51
pignut 78, 100
pike 107
pillwort 135
pimpernel, bog 113
pine 112, 120, 125, 142, 145, 163
   Scots 50, 67, 172
pinewoods 50, 54, 62, 66, 67, 163, 164
Pinnick Wood, New Forest 74
pipit, meadow 84, 141, 169
   tree 142
Pixey Mead, Oxford 80
plankton 15, 107
plantain, water- 126

plover, golden 9, 169
   ringed 18
podsols 138
pollarding 49, 52, 57
pollution 18, 19, 21
   air 52
   marine 18, 19, 21
ponds 106, 144
pondweed, bog 113, 135
ponies 135, 145, 159
poppy, common 96
Portland, Dorset 17
primrose 50, 68
   bird's-eye 80
ptarmigan 169, 174
puffin 19, 29, 30
Purbeck, Isle of 41, 155
purslane, Hampshire 129
puss moth 38

quail 84

rabbits 19, 83, 84, 141, 166, 167
Radipole Lake, Dorset 111
ragged robin 82, 83, 132
ragwort, marsh 83
ramsons 69
Rannoch, Loch 62, 104
Rannoch Moor 121
Rathlin Island 18
rattle, red 113, 132
   yellow 83
raven 167
razorbill 19, 30
redshank 9, 18, 84
redstart 54
   black 7
reed, common 113
reedbed 111
reedswamp 109, 111, 112
reptiles 142, 145
   see also individual species
restharrow, spiny 79
Rhos Fullbrook 132
Ribble, River 15, 119, 129
Ribblesdale 90, 100, 129
rivers 15, 81, 106, 110–11, 119, 129
Robin Hood's Bay 16
rock pools 16, 29
rock-rose 80, 179
   hoary 179
   white 95
Romney Marsh 82
rook 99
rose 90
rosemary, bog 165
Rothiemurchus pine forest 50, 117
rowan 72, 163, 171, 177
Royal Society for Nature
   Conservation 8
Royal Society for the Protection of
   Birds 8, 18, 30, 167
Roydon Common, Norfolk 112
Ruadh-stac-beag 181, 185
rue, meadow 81
rush 81, 121
   blunt-flowered 113
   heath 141
   sea 38
   three-leaved 165

sage, wood 141
St Bees Head 18
St John's wort, bog 113, 132
sallow 145
salmon 21, 106
Saltfleetby, Lincolnshire 39
saltmarsh 16, 21, 35, 109
samphire 16
   golden 35
sand 16, 17, 109, 138, 141
sand-eel 21
sandpiper, common 110
sandstone 18
sandwort, spring 153
sanicle 50
saw-wort 79
saxifrage 165, 182
   starry 183
scabious, devil's-bit 79, 147
Scar Close, Ingleborough 186
schist, Dalradian 166
   mica 182
Schwingmoors 123, 125
Scilly Isles 16
scoter, common 169

Scotland 8, 14, 16–21, 30, 43, 50, 54,
   55, 83, 90, 100, 110, 112, 163, 164,
   165, 166, 167, 169
Scottish Borders 165
Scottish Highlands 166, 167
scree 164
Scridain, Loch 20, 42
scrub 7, 18, 117, 145
   holly 18
sea holly 17
sea lavender 16
sea lettuce 15
sea pea 17, 27
sea rocket 17
sea urchin 43
sea-kale 17, 27
sea-pink *see* thrift
seabird colonies 19, 30
seal 9, 18
   common 18, 34
   grey 18
sedge 17, 112, 113, 120, 121
   bottle 116
   glaucous 80
   pill 141
   pond- 81
   stiff 165
selfheal 83
Selworthy, Somerset 90
Seven Sisters, Sussex 25
Severn Estuary 15, 111
Sgurr Ban 185
shag 19
shearwater, Manx 19
sheep 79, 81, 141, 145, 162, 163, 168
   sheep's-bit 18
shingle 17–18, 27, 35, 109
Shingle Street, Suffolk 27
shrew 166
   water 106
shrike, red-backed 9
Shropshire 108
silver-studded blue 143
silver-Y moth 142
skipper, dingy 98
   silver-spotted 9, 79
skylark 80, 84, 141
snail, water 107
snake, grass 106
   smooth 142
   see also adder
snipe 9, 84
Snowdonia 165
Solway Estuary 15
Somerset 80
Somerset Levels 82, 109
sorrel 83
   sheep's 100, 141
South Stack 18
sparrow, house 7
spearwort, lesser 121
speedwell, heath 141
Spelve, Loch 177
Spey Valley 64, 65, 66, 72, 114, 155,
   162, 172, 177, 185
spider 53, 54, 80, 84, 142, 143, 149
   garden 149
   orb-web 149
   raft 143
   water 106
spurge, sea 34
   wood 50
squill, spring 18, 37
squinancywort 80
squirrel, grey 55
   red 54, 55, 67
stoat 55
stock, sea 41
Stodmarsh, Kent 112
stonechat 142
stonecrop, mossy 141
stonefly 107
Strangford Lough 15
strawberry, wild 98
streams 110–11
Suffolk 48, 109, 111, 141, 146, 154
Suffolk Sandlings 145
sundew 112, 123, 143
   round-leaved 165
Surrey 79, 112, 141, 142, 145
Sussex 79, 145
Sutherland 121, 165, 169
Sutton Holms Meadow, Dorset 93
sweet gale 112
sweet woodruff 50
sycamore 54